MW01124439

My Road Beyond
The Codependent Divorce

Lisa A. Romano

BALBOA.
PRESS
A DIVISION OF HAY HOUSE

ISBN: 978-1-4525-5948-3 (sc)
ISBN: 978-1-4525-5949-0 (e)

Library of Congress Control Number: 2012917766

Balboa Press books may be ordered through booksellers or by contacting:
Balboa Press
A Division of Hay House
1663 Liberty Drive
Bloomington, IN 47403
www.balboapress.com
1-(877) 407-4847

Printed in the United States of America
Balboa Press rev. date: 10/24/12

Author of the Bestselling Book
The Road Back To Me

Acknowledgements

OR OVER THREE DECADES I suffered from amnesia of self. Conditioned by those who were older, stronger and bigger than me, to deny my *self*, I lived the first part of my life asleep and pitifully learned to presume the angst within me was appropriate—and worse that the being I was—was wrong.

Bound no more by the shackles of falsehoods, I have since awakened to self, and have learned to master my own mind. I will be eternally grateful for the spiritual thinkers who have blazed the roads less traveled, for without their insights, my journey might have never begun.

To Gandhi, Socrates, Emerson, Martin Luther King Jr, Plato, Shakespeare, Einstein, Nathaniel Branden, Dale Carnegie, Henry Ford, Merrell-Wolff, Confucius, Wayne Dyer, Anthony De Mello, Melody Beattie, Marianne Williamson, Louise Hay, and to so many, many other teachers of enlightenment who have inspired me to believe in *self*, I thank you—with all that I am.

This book is dedicated to the brokenhearted.

Introduction

M Y FIRST BOOK, *The Road Back To Me* took twelve years to complete. The original draft, which took two years to finish, was lost in a single keystroke. When my computer crashed and my manuscript was sucked into a digital black hole, it took big chunks of my mind with it. Feeling as if the universe had unexpectedly slapped me in the head, I was dazed the moment my monitor faded into nothingness. Stunned by the sudden loss, a deep sense of powerlessness engulfed me as I sat gazing into the black screen. Writing about my life, had become my life. And in one instant it was all gone.

Immediately following the loss of my first manuscript, I considered giving up on the dream of ever being able to help others heal their wounds through the written insights of my personal story. In my heart I firmly believed that the pain I had experienced could be used for the better good, and that the lessons I had learned about codependency and self were ones I needed to share. It wasn't enough that I had learned to live a more stable and satisfying life. I wanted to help change the world. It made no sense to me to keep what I had learned under wraps. Learning to master my own mind saved my life, and I wanted nothing more than to help others learn to do the same. When oblivion claimed my dream, it took all the strength I had not to raise a white flag and ask the universe to leave me alone.

For most of my life I have felt like a square that was desperate to be round. For as long as I can recall I have had an insatiable need to feel as if I belonged—somewhere. It has taken me a lifetime to unwind the prickly strings that have kept my mind bound to thoughts that did little more than reinforce the notion that I was an unworthy being. Faulty childhood programming had solidified deep within my unconscious mind the belief that I was destined to not ever fit in--anywhere.

I was a child when I first discovered I was most at home when words were dancing out of my head and onto stages of white. Expressing my emotions on paper gave them life, and helped me to feel real in a world that so often insisted I not feel what I felt. Writing The Road Back To Me was as cathartic as it was terrifying. Sharing my life story meant I would need to expose the brittle family skeletons the people I loved denied existed at all. For almost two years I wondered when, and if I would ever find the strength to begin facing those bones again. The first go round with those old skeletons had proven to be painful enough.

Two years following the demise of my first manuscript, I began an uphill journey and decided to start writing my story again. Fueled from within by a burning desire to help others learn how to take control over their thoughts, I somehow managed to move beyond my original setback and eventually finished writing my life's story. But completing my manuscript was only act one. My hearts desire to help others learn from my experiences would not be complete until The Road Back To Me was in print, and in the hands of those who might need the encouragement it offered.

Fear of hurting the ones that I loved by exposing my truth is the only reason it took twelve years to finally get my book published. I have since learned to accept that my life's purpose, for whatever reason, is larger than me, and my fears. I am passionate about helping others heal through learning to master the power of their own creative minds. I know healing is possible because I have experienced it first hand, and understand how agonizing facing ones own personal truth can be, especially when those we love are unable to validate for us our very intimate experiences. Thinking and acting according to ones own personal truth is truly a heroic undertaking. Self-mastery requires owning ones own history, in spite of what others prefer we define as reality. But this of course, is not an uncomplicated matter to confront.

It is a miracle my story breaths at all. When I was twelve I tempted suicide. At the time death seemed to be a more pleasing option than life. Exhausted by the need to continuously shield myself from the ones that I loved only made tolerating the repeated bullying I received from the kids at school impossible. As if I were a log being hacked into at both ends, I felt safe nowhere, neither at home nor at school. Death I presumed would at least stop the pain. It was not a bullet that altered my life that day. It was a single positive thought that did.

Many decades later, I find myself humbled by memories of the past. So much of what I have endured now seems so unnecessary, and frivolous even. Time, patience and a commitment to self has taught me to understand that every moment of my life, including the painful ones, were manifestations of what was going on within me on an emotional, and thus a vibrational level. What I thought about, I brought about, and that included all the doom and the gloom. The most difficult part of my journey has been to accept full responsibility for my unhappiness. Once I did not know about this thing called choice. Mastering my own self however, has made it abundantly clear how simple life was intended to be. Reflection not only blankets me with humility, but it also tickles my funny bones.

My books are not written for those interested in collecting data on codependency or for anyone interested in researching case studies on emotional disorders. Although I am confident that anyone interested in understanding the root causes of a conditioned codependent mind would benefit tremendously by coming along for the ride my story offers, I feel it is only fair that I make it perfectly clear that my books are intended for the brokenhearted, and not exclusively for members of clinical communities.

My books are written for people who are struggling to gain control over their lives, and who are in search of a roadmap out of the swamp ones own mind can be. I offer my compelling story up as a beacon of hope for anyone who may be feeling lost within the anxieties of their own thoughts, and who are uncertain as to how to gain control back over their lives. My story is an example of how I slowly learned to tame fear, and to prevail over unconscious dysfunctional childhood programming step-by-step, thought-by-thought, and how I ultimately learned to appreciate the power of creative intent.

I am an author whose greatest desire is to help others bridge within their own consciousness a connection between their inner being and their mind. I have been the self-hating child programmed to believe in her unworthiness. I too have been the anxiety riddled young mother, who regardless of all the things in her life that should have made her happy was deeply unhappy and sadly preoccupied with emptiness. I have spent decades in search of a peace that would never come, believing in ideas that were never my own, and intend to spend the remainder of my life teaching others, through the telling of my own triumphant story, how to look within for the peace that was always there.

My Road—Beyond the Codependent Divorce begins immediately where my first book ended. My family and I are gathered around the kitchen table. We are having spaghetti for dinner. That same afternoon, as I was preparing the meal, Steven offered me an unthinkable ultimatum. Making his position about our relationship abundantly clear, he defiantly announced that he had no intentions of working on our marriage. Dizzying emotions have me by my spine, as I fork spaghetti out of its large bowl and onto the green and white dinner plates that are sitting on the table immediately in front of my three small children and their father. My hands are trembling, and my knees are weak. I understand what Steven's ultimatum means.

There is no time to waste. My body has been failing for years. Asthma is gaining ground. I am tired, debilitated and no longer able to pretend for the sake of white picket fences, and carousels. The walls of my marriage are snuffing the life out of me and my husband has become like an elephant on my chest. I now know what is at the root of our woes. We are a codependent couple playing out our histories. Our only chance of survival lies in our willingness and in our ability to change. It is going to take a commitment from us both to heal who and what we have become, in order to keep our marriage and me alive. Steven's adamant position however, has left me feeling exasperated and without hope.

My teeth are all in place, and my husband has no mistress I know about. My body shows no signs of black and blues. Steven does not drink, smoke or even swear. Our home is custom built, and we have a three-car garage. The pool in our yard is oversized, and our retirement plan is in place. Aware of how perfect my life seems, I have for so long doubted my own right to be unhappy. I can no longer deny the gap between what I see and what I feel. My marriage is terminal, and I know no one I love will agree with my diagnosis. Alone in my newfound awareness, I am struggling to stay detached from the emotions that have been held hostage for so long, as I simultaneously witness what I know will most likely be one of our last spaghetti meals together as a family.

The shit is about to hit the fan, and my innocent babies will not be spared. The glass house they live in that I helped build will soon be shattered, and their mother will be the one wielding the sledgehammer that brought it down. Intellectually I understand what needs to be done. This knowing however, does little to soothe my weeping mothers heart. My children's perfect little lives are about to change forever, and there is nothing I can do to prevent the chaos that is about to come. If I am going to survive, this marriage has to die.

The Ultimatum

THAT SPAGHETTI DINNER SEEMED to last for hours. Steven was clueless. I could tell. His usual silence spoke volumes. He did that when he was angry and disapproved of something I had said. He simply withdrew. I knew Steven assumed the argument we had earlier would eventually blow over, and that soon the dysfunctional balance our relationship had become would be restored.

I was preparing dinner when Steven came home from one of his sessions with his therapist Alice. I was standing at the kitchen sink and straining the spaghetti. I turned towards him when he approached me from behind. He looked angry and his body was tense. Our three babies were on the couch, zoning out in front of the television, doing their best to distract themselves from the impending chaos that was about to unfold a few feet from them. Steam was rising up out of the sink and moistening the back of my t-shirt as Steven began to speak.

"Alice said I don't have to change if I don't want to. So I am not going to change. If you're not happy—you change. And you know what's gonna happen if you keep this shit up Lisa? We're gonna end up getting a divorce because you won't drop this crazy bullshit of yours. Everything is about your feelings, your feelings, your feelings. Ya think most people are happy these days? Nobody is happy these days Lisa. The kind of marriage you want doesn't even exist. But I am warning you...if you don't stop going to this whacko therapist Ed, and if you don't stop reading these self help books, we're gonna wind up getting a divorce. Is that what you want Lisa? You want to get divorced, huh, huh, huh, well do ya?" Steven prodded, his voice growing more intimidating with every syllable.

I'm Not Crazy —
I'm Just Codependent

ONTH'S PRIOR TO THIS showdown I had approached Steven and told him I was unhappy in our marriage. In response, he told me that he thought I was crazy and that I needed to see a shrink.

"Look how you live Lisa. How can you not be happy? There must be something wrong with you. Even your own family thinks you're crazy. You should go see a doctor or something and get your head examined."

Desperate to please my husband, as well as to finally find out once and for all whether or not I really was nuts, I called and scheduled an appointment with a therapist named Ed.

"Why are you here?" Ed asked at our first meeting.

"My husband says I am crazy," I replied.

"Do you think you're crazy Lisa?" he asked.

"I'm not sure. All I know is I'm not happy."

"What would make you happy?"

"I don't feel like my husband and I are on the same page. When I try to talk to him about how I feel, he always tells me I have no right to feel the way I do. He tells me that life shouldn't be about the way I feel. He tells me I should be happy I live in a big house, and that he doesn't cheat on me, and that we have three healthy children. He makes me feel like I don't matter, and yet I worry everyday about how to make his life easier. And when something is bothering him, I am always there for him. So when he calls me names like whacko, psycho, or when he ignores me or says that I am a negative person, it hurts. I feel like he is a stranger to me, but yet he is so happy with the way things are, so I wonder if maybe I am crazy sometimes," I said.

"I didn't ask you what made you unhappy Lisa. I asked you what *would* make you happy," Ed asked.

If my mind was butter, his questions were like a sharp hot knife. As I sat still in my chair, I could feel my thoughts slowing down, and my attention being raised.

"Is there any alcoholism in your family Lisa?"

"My parents don't drink," I replied.

"Listen to my question and answer the question I am asking. Is there any history of alcoholism in your family?"

"Yes. Both sets of my grandparents were alcoholics, and both of my mothers brothers are alcoholics too, but my parents aren't alcoholics," I said.

"I don't remember asking you if your parents were alcoholics," Ed pushed.

"Yes, there is alcoholism in my family," I said.

After a few more questions, and banter back and forth my therapist leaned back in his chair and began to explain what he thought was going on with me.

"I've got some good news and some bad news for you Lisa." Ed said as he knotted his fingers behind his head and stretching to lean back in his chair.

"The good news is you're not crazy. The bad news is you are however co-dependent. Your family has a long history of alcoholism. Your parents are adult children of alcoholics, which is why they were attracted to one another in the first place. More often than not adult children are unaware at how deeply affected they are by their parents alcoholism. Your life is the result of the way you think, and the way you think is the result of your childhood programming, and your programming is the result of whatever your parents programming was. In order for you to truly figure this all out, you'll need to go back to where you began. You have a long road ahead of you, but there is hope. If we can get you to change your thoughts, we can change your life," he said.

Unsure of what his diagnosis meant, but certain I had no place else to turn, I made the decision to commit myself to learning all I could about this thing called codependency. My life was falling apart around me, and I was discovering how few coping skills I had to handle the strain of shattered dreams. My only hope was that my therapist was right and I wasn't crazy.

Immediately following my first therapy session I bought the book called *Codependent No More* by Melody Beattie. While reading the opening chapter, I felt an unfamiliar feeling rising within my chest. With every sentence my heart seemed to pick up its pace. As if the sentiments expressed had been plucked out of my mind, my being felt mysteriously at home. Spooked by the oddity of suddenly feeling at home, at one point I slammed the book shut. This author knew me, and deeper she understood me. Feeling known was as terrifying as it was welcoming.

As I continued reading about the nature and root causes of codependency, I began to comprehend the idea that if I didn't give up, I would one day be free of this insidious psychological disposition. I wondered who I might be once I stopped blaming others for my unhappiness, and I once and for all, took ownership over my right to be happy. Too tired of what my life had become, I forged ahead hoping that Steven would be as excited about changing our lives for the better as I was.

Within a few days of reading *Codependent No More*, my eyes had already begun to shed their distorted lenses. Although it was still very early in my recovery, I had faith that my therapy sessions, coupled with what I was learning on my own time about codependency, would one day pay off, and I would eventually live a healthier life. The most difficult aspect of my early recovery was learning to accept that the ones I loved, including Steven, didn't have to change. Even more difficult to learn to accept, was the idea that I didn't have to worry about how the ones that I loved felt about my decision to change my life. So ingrained with the sense that everything I did, felt, or thought needed to be approved by others, learning to detangle my mind from its childhood programming, made my mind feel as if it was in mental boot camp.

The Codependent Us

MY BACK WAS GETTING wet. The steam from the spaghetti was hot, and Steven had successfully positioned himself close enough to me so that slipping away from the sink would have been an aggressive and awkward move. My heart thumped wildly as I stood and looked deeply into his cocoa colored eyes. My spirit knew the man that I loved was lost somewhere deep within the complex oasis his mind had become. Between us there was only this thing—this dynamic—this way of relating called codependency, and for me it was no longer enough, and worse—it was killing me.

"Is that what you want Lisa? You want a divorce?" Steven asked me again, only this time raising his voice. Before answering I once again glanced over at my three children who were slipping into safe trance like states. I could relate. I did that too when I was a child, whenever my life was about to get turned upside down.

Therapy had taught me much about codependency in the recent months. I now understood that Steven and I were repeating the codependent patterns we had learned as children, and that in turn he and I were conditioning our children with the same dysfunctional belief systems. I knew that unless I changed something, nothing would change, and that as a result my children might one day be locked inside similar dysfunctional patterns. Fueled by my commitment to spare them the type of trauma I was now experiencing, I swore to myself I would do whatever I had to do to ensure my children would one day live healthy and self fulfilled codependent free lives.

Looking up at my husband, I struggled to accept, that he would not be able to understand the words that were about to come out of my mouth.

"No Steven I don't want a divorce. I need a divorce. Alice is right. You don't have to change. That is your right. But I have rights too. And I have the right to want more out of a marriage. I know now that I cannot change you. I was wrong to try. I am sorry. I am sorry I am not what you want me to be. And I am sorry, but you are not what I want you to be. I am sorry I enabled you. I am sorry I worried so much about what you thought about me. I should have not made you responsible for my happiness. I was wrong to expect you to make me feel worthy. It was never your job to give me what I should have been able to give my self," I said, clearly, decisively and as if my spirit herself were speaking.

Steven stretched his head back, looked from side to side, and said,

"You're nuts Lisa."

The Witness

PRESSED PIECES OF SPAGHETTI were dripping from Niccole's hair. Amanda's dainty fingers were rosy red and Max had stained his new white t-shirt with tomato sauce. None of those things irked me now like they had in the past. Thoughts raced through my mind like a swarm of bees, as I sat observing my small children delightfully enjoying the last bits of their meal.

I am quickly becoming aware of how many tender moments I have lost to dysfunctional thinking. Awareness is as bitter as it is soothing. I am not just the mouse with her tail caught in the trap. I am the trap, the cheese, and the observer of it all. I understand now how limited my ping pong ball sized awareness has always been, and I am struggling to integrate the consequences of my thinking. I know why I am where I am, and truer, I now humbly understand I am the creator of the stabbing reality I am observing in the moment.

Soon my children, Steven and I would be swept up like bits of unsuspecting pieces of sand on a shore. To take my family where I needed it to go, meant that the family we were needed to be destroyed. Divorce, like chemotherapy, harms for the sake of the good. My codependent life—the result of living in a skewed reality—shame based—and perfectionistic world must be leveled and cleared away in order for me to begin restructuring my mind. I am full of fear, but understand that without fear there is no courage.

In my mind I hear my spirit urging me not to give up. I imagine what it is I would want my children to do if they were where I was now, and struggle not to get swept off of my feet by the swirling emotional undertow that is yanking at my limbs.

Emotional Chemo

MAX, AMANDA AND I were standing in the playroom that leads to the garage. My babies, drenched in teary pajamas, and consumed with anxiety had followed Steven there. Their father didn't pack any of his things. As if my family and I had suddenly morphed onto a carcass littered battlefield, my mind searched for a place to protect my children from the assaults of this inconspicuous war. I felt powerless to shield them from the wounds they were suffering, as they witnessed their daddy walk out the door.

A vicious argument between Steven and our eleven-year old son Max had been the catalyst for his leaving that night, only a few short weeks after that spaghetti dinner. The spine tingling explosiveness between them had proven to be the straw that broke our family's fragile camels back.

That night started out like so many of the others. Drained emotionally and physically by the sharp sudden blows of my marriages demise, asthma and a jabbing migraine headache had followed me to bed. Confident that my inhaler was within my reach, I did my best to lay my beaten head onto my pillow, in hopes that the coming nights hours would not leave me gasping for air. As slumber began to fall, a sudden and cold jolt of adrenaline shocked my heart into a panicked rhythm.

"Die, daddy die. I want you to die."

The frustration in my eleven-year-old sons voice summoned me to my feet. I found Steven standing over Max, who was seated Indian style on the floor next to his bed.

"Go ahead. You wanna hit me, ya wanna hit me?" Steven was yelling, stooping down at Max, with the sound of blood dripping in his voice. Both of his fists were clenched.

I stood in the doorway of Max's bedroom and was horrified at the heart ringing vision in front of my eyes. My family was falling apart. And worse, I was alone in this perception. Steven couldn't see it. He had long forgotten all about our spaghetti dinner.

For months I had urged Steven to pay attention to what the animosity between he and I was doing to our children. I often asked that he not oppose me in front of them. I feared that our children would absorb the tension that was churning about in our home, and that eventually symptoms of our marital breakdown would surface in them in one form or in others. In my gut I sensed that Steven was taking much of his frustrations about our failing marriage out on our son, and that Max may have even been able to sense this was true. A proud little boy, our son, like his mother never liked being pushed around, and especially unfairly.

Reality grabbed a hold of my spine and demanded attention. I could no longer pretend that my children were not being affected by the tension between their father and I, even if Steven preferred to hold tomatoes in front of his eyes. By that time Steven and I had been arguing regularly. And if we weren't arguing, we were ignoring one another instead.

More than once our children had overheard Steven menace me with divorce. My attempts to communicate with the father of my children always ended with threats. Steven got angry whenever I attempted to express my desire to improve our marriage. And I got angry too. For many years my heart felt alone in a relationship built for two. Afraid the extra weight I had been carrying might eventually suffocate life from me soon, I was now convinced that a divorce was my only chance for survival. Asthma, migraine headaches, and unexplained rashes had made my body their homes.

Shortly before that explosive night, I had begun to notice how each of my children's moods changed whenever Steven came home. As if my children had heard the sounding of an alarm, and were now suddenly hypersensitive to their environments, my children were being changed by the changes in their home. I knew the moment I saw Steven leaning over Max things had gone too far. Evidence our family dynamic had gone rogue, I feared Max was suffocating too.

Without time to think, I jumped in between them, and pulled Max close. He was trembling from fear and I was sure grief too. This straw was not his fault, and I hoped with all of my heart that I would be able to convince my innocent son that whatever was happening in our home had nothing to do with him. His father and I, and the way we related to one another was ill, not him, not my little boy.

The oceans of emotions within me that I had for so long attempted to keep calm, barreled out of me like a tsunami that evening, as I held Max in my arms. This wasn't about the tuna fish can Max decided to open up that night, or about the fact that Steven was just frustrated that Max was hungry at that hour, or that Max was cranky and had answered his father back in a disrespectful way.

As Max and I fused into a crying ball Steven began to offer what seemed to be half-hearted apologies. Steven towered over my son and I. From above me and through my rain soaked eyes, and through Max's belly cries, I could hear Steven fumble with his words.

"Okay, Okay just relax. It's no big deal. Max your mom and I don't want you eating tuna fish late at night because you already had dinner. Stop crying now. I said I am sorry," he said. But as time ticked on, and neither Max nor I met Steven half way, Steven's disposition began to change.

"Lisa, stop babying this kid will you! You're going to turn him into a sap! You know what? I think you're both nuts. What's wrong with you two?" he continued, his fence walking words only adding more fuel to the fire that raged in my ornery guts.

Casualties of War

TRYING HARD NOT TO fade into black, I did my best to stand tall as the bullets began to fly. If it is possible to have your heart break, and yet for it to continue to beat, then that is what happened to me the night I watched Steven walk out the door. Max and Amanda were terrified. I could see it in their eyes. Steven was just as frightened, and confused as our children. I could see that in his eyes too. If there was a light at the end of the tunnel, I couldn't see it now. My babies were having their eyes scooped out and in many ways I was doing the scooping.

My children and I didn't sleep much that night. After heavy bouts of crying in the playroom behind our garage door, I took them both by their hands and lead them to their rooms. Neither of my children wanted to sleep alone. With Max tucked beneath one of my arms, and Amanda under the other, the three of us tried not to wake Niccole who had somehow slept through the ruckus. Through sniffles and weeps, and through tears and hiccups, my babies and I struggled to find a sense of balance as we lay in my bed.

I did my best to help my children understand that what had happened that night had nothing to do with them. I bumbled my way towards an explanation of the truth I hoped their young minds would be able to comprehend. Still early on in my recovery from codependency, I had yet to fully understand the emotional disease myself. What was clear however, was the fact that I was no longer going to ignore what I thought was wrong. And no matter how difficult it was going to be, somehow I would find the strength to heal my codependent mind so that I could model for my children, a life worth living.

Max and Amanda asked me questions I could not answer. They wondered if their daddy was coming back, and if Steven and I were going to get a divorce. They asked if Steven was going to be angry when he came home, or if he was going to be a nice daddy when he did. They asked if their grandparents were going to come to our house anymore. They asked me where we were going to live if daddy never came back. They asked me if they could take their bicycles to wherever we were going to go. They wondered about what their friends were going to say to them about their daddy moving out. They said they didn't want anyone to know that their daddy and mommy might be getting a divorce. And as I cradled the innocent victims of the havoc my life had created, I begged God to give me the courage to find the words that I could only hope would ease their pummeled souls, as the mommy in me gasped for air.

I wished I could shake Steven and wake him up. I had for so long believed in his greatness, and often told him that I did. Steven was lost inside his own faulty beliefs. I hoped for many years, that one day Steven would finally 'get it', and live in the moment with me. I was beginning to understand that-that was what was wrong. It was never my responsibility to get Steven to change or 'see it' at all.

Lisa A. Romano

He had a right to believe what he wanted, even if what he thought he wanted was based on dysfunctional belief systems, and was not what I wanted for our relationship. And I, regardless of how difficult it would be to assert my right, had a right to end a marriage that I knew was only perpetuating the cycle of codependency. If Steven wasn't willing to change what we had become, then that meant our family had no other choice but to face the tornados of divorce, because I was not willing to die physically, mentally or spiritually. Nor was I willing to indoctrinate my children with the same codependent belief systems that had for so long diseased my mind, and my body. Deeper, I no longer had the stamina to get Steven to want to see what I saw, or to get him to hear what I was saying. My soul had been exhausted.

I was born into a codependent institution, and therefore had been taught to disown my own self, and to worry more about what others needed than what I needed. I had been conditioned to think that my happiness was dependent on how well I could make others feel. I was programmed to attune myself to the whims of others, and as a result never learned to connect to my 'self', or to satisfy my own emotional needs. I was taught to tolerate emotional and verbal abuse, and to instead swallow any impulse to defend my 'self'. Without a right to self, defending the spirit within was an impossible notion to assert.

On the surface I felt like a victim, but in truth, I was as guilty as any character in my life now. In all of my caretaking was the need to feel worthy. My caring for others, was not as authentic as I had falsely once believed it was. And now, after many years of playing a game I was unaware I had been playing, I was done. Steven had not met my unspoken expectations. I was more than willing to cater to my husband, but in return he would adore me, and fill up all those empty holes in my soul. And when he failed to meet my unconscious demands, I would whimper and whine and complain about how hard I had worked to please him. I was codependent, and unknowingly operating under the illusion of a belief system I had been programmed and conditioned to accept as truth.

Therapy had opened my eyes to 'self'. It was never just Steven's fault, or my parent's fault. I was as much to blame for the turmoil my soul was in as anyone in my life. And now that I understood what was at the heart of my problem, I wanted nothing more but to begin thinking better thoughts. I knew that if my husband could open his mind to the information I had so easily accepted, our marriage could survive. But I also knew, that if Steven shut down, and refused to expand his awareness of self, I would have to leave my marriage, and take my children on a stormy unpredictable ride.

My babies deserved better than Steven, and better than me. They deserved two parents who did not rely on anyone but their selves for personal happiness. They deserved parents who did not need to manipulate feelings of worthiness out of others, who did not play the victim or need to induce guilt to get others to do what they unconsciously believed they needed them to do. I could see my lack now. I could see how dysfunctional my thoughts once were, and I wanted nothing more than to scrub my subconscious mind of all its faulty childhood programming, so that I could assure I was not going to make the same innocent mistakes my parents had in their rearing of me.

If my children were going to have a fighting chance at a healthy non-codependent life, it was going to be up to me to somehow bite through these chains without the support of their father. The people I shared my life with, as far as I could tell, were all codependent. I didn't know anyone who had a loving marriage, or who wasn't self destructive in some way shape or form. I felt surrounded by control freaks, complainers, workaholics, alcoholics, gamblers, liars, cheaters, and people pleasers. And I was the biggest black kettle. The road ahead would undoubtedly be littered with potholes of many shapes, sizes, and depths. I had a burning desire that one day my children might be spared of codependent belief systems and dysfunctional thinking. The hopes I had for the future lives of my children helped to at least light the path ahead.

Night blended into morning, and as it did the suns rays began to filter through my Pella window blinds. As the rays danced like light-toed fairies on my tear soaked cheeks, I forced my mind to focus on the warmth it brought to my face, trying hard to stay grateful for something. My babies would soon awaken to discover, that the nightmare they had witnessed was not a dream. Daddy was gone, and so was the life they once knew.

Tuning In Meant Tuning Out

L IVING WITH STEVEN HAD become like living with gangrene. It never got better. It only got worse. I am sure he felt the same way about me. Years of me putting my needs last had left me dry. Robotic almost, especially around him, I knew he perceived me as the only one with the issue. He presumed that his moving out, the selling of our home, and our looming divorce was entirely my fault. In his mind, he could not comprehend how or why what was happening was taking place. Many times I felt as if Steven and I spoke different languages, and as if we truly were from different galaxies.

"I'm happy Lisa. You're not, so you're the one with the problem," he used to say. "If you feel crazy, then you really should go to a psychiatrist. I am not unhappy. I like things just the way they are," were common comments of his.

It was a familiar sense. I cried myself to sleep many nights wondering if he were right. Did I have the right to not be happy in spite of how perfect things looked on the outside? Did I have the right to expect my husband to consider my feelings or to at least act like how I felt mattered? Did I have the right to get angry when he pretended not to hear me, or he claimed to forget the things that we agreed upon? Did I have a right to feel impatient with him when he failed to do what he said he was going to do? Did I have the right to not want to have sex with him because I felt more like a mother to him than a wife? Perhaps my mother was right. Maybe I was selfish. Maybe I was a schizophrenic like my Aunt Evelyn. Everyone around me seemed so content in his or her perceptions of the world we shared, that quite often, I wondered what was wrong with me.

The maybe's were behind me, or at the very least had taken a back seat to what was happening in my turbulent now. The night Steven left I knew my life had come down to do or die. As I did my best to brace for my marriages fall, I struggled to remind myself that I had turned over every stone in an effort to save it. And as Steven, his family and even my own family began to shake their disapproving fingers my way, it was hellish at times to get out of bed to face another day. Years prior, my body had begun its revolt. In addition to the emotional stress of my separation, I was also dealing with a plethora of physical illnesses, that my doctors assured me were the results of chronic anxiety.

I had repressed too much for too long. Steven didn't see it. Steven didn't care. Steven was incapable of meeting me halfway. He was happy, and that gave him the right to not see me in his mind. But I knew better, even if my soul had not found the strength or the words to say it. Steven was happy because I made his happiness a priority. I *saw* Steven. The problem was, I *saw* everyone--even the ones who couldn't see me.

Learning to hear my *self* was just the beginning. Feeling deaf within my own being to my inner self, was the norm. Turning up the volume within me, was only half of the equation. I would also need to learn how to tune others out, especially now as the cyclones of change began to twist. This would not be easy. My entire life had been built on my ideas of what others thought about me. The sea of my life had been a churning one. I didn't know it, but the boat my life was in had always been headed in the wrong direction. Pretending I knew where I was going was a memory now. As my dependency on lung expanding medications increased, so did my newfound personal convictions.

In codependent terms, the tuning out I was learning to do was called detachment. So foreign the idea of turning my focus away from what others wanted, needed, or expected of me, I often felt much like a leaf caught up in a thunderstorm. Where would I go without worrying about others needs? Who would I be if I were not overly concerned about rescuing or changing others? How would I spend my days without obsessing over how to convince others my life was perfect? Not worry about Steven? Not worry what he thought about me? Not worry about what my parents were going to feel or what the neighbors were going to say about Steven moving out, or about the selling of our home? In the early days of my recovery, I was so codependent that I worried about not worrying.

It Is What It Is

"You're out. You better go find a place for you and the kids to live," Steven said, as our three babies stood by my side.

The kids and I had just returned from Rosey's house. I was surprised to find Steven in the kitchen. I tried not to act stunned when I walked into our home and noticed the red suit jacket sitting at our dining room table. I knew who she was. Her real estate billboards were all over town.

Uncomfortable, the real estate agent bid her farewells and left a neat pile of papers on my kitchen counter.

"Good luck with everything Mrs. Romano," she said, brushing my arm on her way out.

Steven was irritated. It was easy to see. His brows were stern, and his passive aggressive persona was in full bloom.

"So…did my kiddies have a good time at Rosey's?" he asked, in his confusing, condescending tone. "Aww— that's good. Daddy is so, so, happy you're happy," he continued as he raised our youngest daughter up and in for a hug.

"I hope mommy can find you guys a house with a pool like we have now. Right mommy? Won't you find a house with a big pool for the kids to play in once we are divorced? That's what you want right mommy? You want a divorce? You want to break up our family right mommy? Mommy doesn't like living with daddy kids, so we're going to have to sell the house, right mommy?" Steven continued on relentlessly, as the blood in my veins began to heat up.

"Things are alright kids, don't worry. Mommy and daddy will figure this all out, and eventually things will get better, right daddy?" I said trembling, as he drizzled acid on all of our open wounds.

On this terrain Steven was a much more agile warrior than I. His defenses and attacks were akin to a seasoned military man. As if my mind were a minefield, Steven knew just where to step to cause an explosion in my head. I knew he'd never understand that in all his sarcasm he was scarring our children. And worse, even if he did realize he was hurting them, he'd blame me for his lack of self-control anyway.

It was almost impossible not to unravel in front of Steven and the kids. This was really happening. We were selling the house. Steven really had moved out, and we really were on our way towards a divorce. My mind wanted to run. But I wasn't sure where. That was common. I didn't think my thoughts. My thoughts always thought me. Like mud sliding down a hill, my toxic thoughts gathered up momentum and blanketed me in thick muck. Overloaded with emotion, and slightly fearful of Steven's mounting rage, I gathered the kids up and loaded them back into our minivan.

"You know what kids? I think I forgot my sunglasses at Rosey's house," I said, as I nudged my three children back down the stairs, and out through our garage door.

At Rosey's, I sipped on green tea and told her that Steven had put the house on the market without me knowing. My childhood chum wasn't surprised. I secretly hoped she hadn't yet grown tired of my children and I. We had spent the entire day with her and her children at her home.

"He wants you to be afraid. He wants to push this as far as he can, because he thinks you'll buckle and go back to him. He thinks he can push you around and bully you into staying married to him, even though you're not happy and your relationship sucks. In his mind, because you have such a nice house, you have no right *not* to be happy. Lisa, he doesn't want to change. He doesn't know how to change, and it's obvious – he doesn't see you. It is what it is," she said.

Rosey's matter of fact demeanor was as welcomed as it was confusing. Although Rosey was correct in her assumptions about Steven, her no frills analysis of my life left me feeling dizzy. I wished I could think the way she did. The colossal weight of my emotions seemed almost foolish in contrast to her interpretations of my collapsing life.

Glancing over at each of my children, I wondered if she understood how deeply my heart and mind had been aching for the misery my children had been going through. Too, I wondered if in her pragmatic views, she comprehended how wretched their life was about to become. There seemed nothing simple, or prosaic about their life or mine now.

"What are you crying about now?" Rosey asked, as my souls marrow cracked beneath the strain of umpteen fears.

The Cats Out of The Bag

THE WOMAN IN THE red suit jacket told Steven it could take many months to sell our home. I was relieved almost, because since signing our real estate contract life seemed to warp into hyper drive. The newness was terrifying. And although on an intellectual level I understood that Steven and I had to get a divorce, my emotional side was sinking to her knees. Steven wasn't happy, and he wasn't very nice when he was angry. As a codependent I feared others anger, and was now coming face to face with the results of the years of enabling I had been a part of in my relationship with Steven.

Steven stood in front of our large French doors. The sign had just been delivered. Busying myself nervously in the kitchen, I heard him say, "Wow you're really going to go through with this huh Lisa? You really are going to keep going to therapy, and you're going to keep reading those psycho self-help books of yours aren't ya? You should kiss my feet. Who do you know who lives like this Lisa? Even your parents think you're nuts. It's not me-it's you. You're crazy. I can't believe you haven't come to your senses yet. This is gonna get ugly you know."

As I leaned into my dishwasher to grab hold of a clean glass, I could hear myself repeat over and over in mind "Hold onto your self. Hold onto your self. Hold onto your self." Tuning in while tuning out, I did my best not to dance with the grim reaper called fear.

It felt like my panties and bras were being hung out for the world to see. The red, white and blue real estate sign flapped in the wind like a goddamn press release. The gabby neighborhood would soon know that Steven and I were getting a divorce, and I knew none of them would understand why. My therapist had warned me not to 'attach' myself to worrying about what other people thought, and to especially stay detached from what I thought they thought about me. But as the fabrications my in-laws began to spread like smoke in the air, the life I once lived slipped like grains of sand into a gritty mirage. Nothing was comfortable or recognizable about my life now. I struggled greatly to go deeper within my own self, to find the balance only my divine and rooted spirit could offer me, as my physical world began crashing to the ground below on which my feet stood, like rain made of sharpened glass.

Why I Am
Who I Am

SINCE STEVEN HAD MOVED out, my parents had pulled away. They thought that I was wrong for wanting a divorce, and blamed me for the separation. I had attempted many times to tell them that Steven was the one who had given up, and that he was the one who told me 'to get a fucking attorney', but they never heard me. They adored Steven, and Steven adored them, and in addition to their mutual admiration, my mom and dad were a codependent king and queen, who didn't care much for wrinkles or frowns.

It was my fault and I knew it. Ed was right. My life was a puzzle, and as much as it disgusted me to admit it, it was I who constructed it all. I had played the game too. I was in codependent recovery now, and there was nowhere to hide. For so long I had been that little girl who feared making others angry, aware that daddy preferred smiles, and that mommy preferred it when daddy was happy, I unknowingly had played into their illusions. I knew marrying a man like Steven made my parents proud of me. I was struggling now to accept that my choice to marry him was very much the result of an unconscious codependent need of mine to gain my parents validation. The awareness made me feel like I was rubbing vinegar in my own eye.

Many times during my marriage I wished I could pick up the phone and call one of my parents to tell them the truth. I wished I could go grab a cup of coffee with my mom, and tell her that I was struggling with my feelings for Steven. I wished I felt like daddy's little girl, and that my happiness was all that mattered to him. But I knew that my parents considered feelings inconvenient, and deeper, I did not know how to tell them the truth. Fear of disappointing them always overshadowed my ability to be authentic with them, and even with my own self.

My mother and father were stunned when I told them that Steven had moved out.

"I am not happy daddy. I can't take it anymore. Steven and I are going to get a divorce," I said, shaking from the fear of disappointing him.

His face melted into a mask of dismay.

"Lisa, Lisa, Lisa, what the hell are you thinking? You don't have to be happy. Who is happy? Do you think your mother and I are happy? You just have to survive. Life is hard Lisa. And how are you going to make it on your own with three kids without a man in your life? You can't move back in here you know. What are you going to do?" he said.

My father could never have known it, but what he said to me that day made me more convinced than ever that I was doing the right thing. I was nervous, rickety, and even petrified about what might happen next, but certain for sure I had to keep going. Clearer than ever, I could see how fear-based my father's whole life had been. My father's priority was never happiness. He didn't even believe in it. My father's agenda was status quo. It wasn't about feeling alive. It was about staying alive. It wasn't about love. It was about fear. My father's life was built on dread. Fearful of chaos, daddy sought to control all that he could, including his and our messy emotions. I couldn't blame him. He was a little boy whose mother committed suicide when he was four, and whose father was a violent alcoholic.

I felt sorrow for his wife, my mother who had given up her life for a man who didn't believe in happiness. I empathized with the woman my mother had become, who had not been loved from the inside out like she deserved to have been by a man who was not afraid to love with all of his being. On many occasions when I was a child, I'd wish my father would wrap my mother in his arms and make her feel like a woman who was adored by a man. I needed to see my father love, as well as see my mother feel loved. But all I could see were white walls.

Even though I loved my parents, I eventually learned to pity them. What they taught me, was not right, and it wasn't fair. But most of all, it wasn't their fault. They did the best they could, but that didn't change the fact that a relationship like theirs was exactly what I didn't want.

It was a titanic boulder off of my back and thus a mammoth relief. With my parents pulling away, it became one less vat of soup I needed to keep endlessly stirring. With my children's lives coming undone, my instincts to protect them overrode the hemorrhaging childhood wounds of my past. Their pulling away was in many ways an unexpected gift. It was my responsibility now to undo what had been done. With less pus of my past getting in the way now, I was beginning to appreciate the distance.

At one of my therapy session I told Ed about the meeting I had had with my parents. His shoebox-sized office had become my sanctuary. By this time in my recovery, I had come to understand that Ed wasn't there to judge me. He was there to help facilitate the re-birthing of my lost self.

"How did your parents react when you told them Steven moved out?" Ed asked. "Well my mother didn't say anything at all. Her disapproving facial expressions spoke for her. My father however, made it clear he thought I was making a mistake. He told me I didn't have to be happy," I said.

"And how do you feel about that statement?"

With an oven full of desire in my heart, and an ever-expanding smile growing upon my face, I said, "I am happy I am me."

"That's really good Lisa, really good," Ed said, as a not so familiar smile seeped across his face. My thoughts were changing. I could feel my mind reaching beyond the barriers of what once was. And life, although had become like an abyss, I was learning to trust guidance from within.

Getting My
History Straight

MY DEPRESSION DIDN'T CEASE when Steven moved out, or when the house went up for sale. In fact, in many ways my depression worsened. Thankful for Ed, who specialized in the area of codependency, I had grown to rely on our weekly Tuesday sessions. He encouraged me to journal everyday and as often as I could, and especially when I didn't feel like doing it. He said that in time telling my truth would get easier to do, and that eventually the depression would lift.

In the wee hours of the morning, and before the kids rustled out of bed, I would drag my dense body to the kitchen and brew myself an entire kettle of green tea, that I inevitably would consume before my journaling sessions were through. For some peculiar reason, I looked forward to sipping green tea alone, and by candlelight. I did not question the peculiarity. I went with it instead.

Depression made me feel like I was wearing a wet grizzly bears coat. I felt like my head was full of golf ball sized rocks, and like my belly was full of swampy sand. A monumental chore to even get my feet to touch the floor after I opened my eyes in the a.m., some mornings all I really wanted to do was wilt away under my comforter, for maybe one day or two. A reprieve is what I needed, not only from what was seeping up out of me, but from what was being thrown at me as well.

It was like trying to see through smoky cracked glass. Sometimes the tears that dripped out of my soul were so many, that by the time my journaling jags were through, the pages of my journal resembled tie-dyed ink splatters. Occasionally the paper I was writing on would become so tear soaked, that I'd have to jump to the next clean page, because I'd cried the paper too thin.

On mornings when I felt too weak to write, I would remember the advice I was paying Ed for.

"Lisa, in order for you to free yourself you are going to have to figure out what got you stuck in the first place," Ed said, in more ways than one, and more than once.

"Stick with the journaling, and don't give up. You're just digging for the pieces of the puzzle now. Eventually we'll be able to piece them together, and you will not only see who you've become, but you'll also get to decide who you want to be," he would continue, and repeat, continue and repeat.

I had very few places to turn to now. My parents, my brother Marc and my sister Leslie's lack of concern for my situation with Steven, made me feel unloved. Their distance spoke volumes, and my spirit was too flimsy to beg for their understanding. Consumed with fear of the unknown, and guilt ridden for the trauma Steven was creating in my children's lives, it was a triumph to be able to get through the day without a full blown panic attack. My children remained my main concern. And although they were, I never lost the aching for my maternal families support.

Rosey was right. It was what it was. But between the accepting of what my marriage had become and the surrendering to what my marriage had become was a wide sea of emotional stuff I didn't know how to swim in yet. Void of coping skills, and aware that without them I'd never be able to cross the grand divide and reach the promise land in my mind, I clung to the wisdom Ed offered each week as if it were Manna being sent from the heavens.

And so, with marble notebooks and pens in tow, the love for the future lives of my children became the impetus I needed to call to my hearts stage, all the painful emotions I had so long ago stowed away. Although the connection I had to my higher self was still spindly, it was enough for me then. Newly aware that I could observe my thoughts without attaching emotionally to them, my candlelit early morning journaling jags became like life rafts in the watery divide that separated me from acceptance and surrender in the choppy waters of my laden mind.

I didn't know where I was going. All I knew was that I couldn't stay. I didn't know what I was doing wrong. But I knew that what I was doing wasn't right. I didn't know what I'd find when I found surrender. But I did know that unless I learned to accept my fears about all the unknowns, I'd never be able to transfer my children from here to there.

Paper and pen helped siphon me dry. And as the many candlelit mornings turned into many days, I learned to trust Ed's guidance. In spite of how wretched remembering was, I always felt slightly lighter by the time my green tea was through.

The Stories Tears Tell

"WHAT DO YOU WANT to do with the rest of your life Lisa?"

My father and I were sitting in the basement at our small kitchenette. I was about seventeen.

"I want to be a writer," I said, secretly wishing my father would offer me the encouragement I needed.

"No—no—no you don't want to be a writer. You'll never make any money as a writer. You want to be a nurse. People always die," he said, as he shook his head from side to side, making me feel as if my desires were silly and perhaps frivolous too.

It has been a lifelong dream of the giant little girl I am, to make her daddy happy. As a child, I would try to quiet the first man that I ever loved whenever he got upset. When he responded as I hoped and anticipated, I would feel better. The fear of rejection that burned like a campfire in the pit of my soul would calm. In the calming of my father, I discovered I could calm myself too.

"You is an ugly child. Who could your momma be? If I were your daddy, I'd go jump in the sea."

It was a tune my father would sing often around the house. His pitch was jovial, and his face always wore a grin. He never sang it when he was angry. As a child I knew he thought he was being funny. I knew he wanted his children to think that too, but I never did. Not really anyway. I smiled regardless.

My heart would break for Marc. When we were children, my father had little patience for Marc's less than perfect school reports or homework assignments.

"You stupid ass. What the hell are you doing? You're friggin lazy!" my father would shout, dressed in his uniform white tank top and pressed blue jeans.

I weep still for the little boy Marc was, who like me, wished only to please his daddy. Fear, anger, sadness and guilt would well up inside me as I witnessed Marc begin to unwind under our fathers verbal assaults. Marc's shoulders would round over his marble notebooks, as he stretched his eyes in attempts to prevent the tears from ruining his homework. He had been singled out. I could feel his embarrassment, his feelings of unworthiness, his aching for approval, and even disgust for his own lack. I stuffed the empathy I had for his pain inside of me, somewhere between a cloud and the ground.

I loved and hated the man who was hurting my brother. I yearned and despised my need for his approval. I loved the little brother I knew who didn't love me. And I wished from my toes that Marc knew what I knew.

"Look at Lisa's work. See how neat her homework is? If she can do it so can you," my father would spew adding only to Marc's growing distain for his older sister. I hated when my father did that to Marc. And I hated when he did that to me. My need for my father's approval was as breath stealing as a plastic bag over my face.

Alone in my perceptions and denied their validation, I learned to not feel worthy of my experiences.

As my life with Steven came unglued, I found myself face to face with the crux of one of my many childhood wounds, much to the thanks of journaling. Fear of rejection had played a colossal role in my life, and more so than I had ever assumed. Fear had been as much a part of my existence as the blood in my veins. Like an emotional tool, fear was used to manipulate the being I was into place, according to the whims of others.

My father had few psychological tools in his emotional shed. He could have never known that his beliefs regarding the rearing of his children were all faulty and did little more than infect his offspring with the idea that they were not worthy beings. When my father sang me that song, and when I was made to wonder if I were ugly, and if I were worthy of love, he was unaware how wretched the ringing of his rhyme had been on my skimpy soul.

My father disliked boisterous, confident children, and he was not intimidated to offer his verbal disapproval of any child he noticed that he deemed as one who was 'showing off' or who appeared to be 'cocky'. In the chopping away of his children's self esteem, was his desire to prevent us from ever being judged by others as possibly being labeled as conceited little children too. Blended well within the weave of deprecating frowns, and critical analysis of others, were the rules of conformity Marc, Leslie and I learned to obey.

"If you wanna' cry, go upstairs and cry," my father would say, if ever one of us slipped through an invisible crack.

It was not safe to trust or to love, to laugh or to cry, to want or to need, to live or to die. My father needed walls. Unable to connect to his own feelings, meant he was unable to allow his children to connect to theirs. Another consequence of the barriers he built, meant his children could never find him, or that he could ever find them. Perhaps the most troubling consequence of all, was that my father was contently unaware anything was missing.

I was struggling to trust my feelings now, the ones that paper and pen were helping me to reveal. As our real estate sign flapped in the winds, and as the parent's I didn't know began to whisper behind my back at my children's school, and as my father and mother continued to withdraw from me, doubt sometimes consumed me like a pack of starved carnivores. My now, the results of the cumulative thoughts of all of my yesterdays, sometimes made me feel like there were wolves chomping at my heels.

Journaling, although I came to respect its cathartic results, was more faceted than I ever appreciated before. The deep wounds I kept finding would not heal overnight. This journey I was on towards health had many doors that needed to be found before they could be opened. Accepting I was unhappy was just the beginning. Allowing myself to feel what I felt was still just another step along the way. Learning to trust what I found was another.

Getting divorced was akin to playing Russian roulette with the only life I had ever known. As dysfunctional as it was, I didn't know anything else. What I craved was all in my head. I knew I wanted something more, but had no experience of what I dreamed of. Trusting my hopes for a better future, as well as trusting my current perceptions felt like I was walking on a bed of nails, barefoot and in the rain. I felt lost, unsure, and many times inundated with fear.

Divorcing Steven meant I was divorcing my father, or at least my childhood needs that were at the saddle of so many of my fears. Fear was just getting in the way now. I needed to move on. I had to learn to let go of my fear of displeasing my father, and accept that in the living of my own life, it was quite possible my father would in fact abandon me. In so many ways however, he already had.

Displeasing my father meant I gambled with his acceptance. Rolling the dice on his acceptance meant possibly encountering his rejection. At the helm of many of my turbulent storms was an ingrained sense of trepidation that was directly linked to a fear of abandonment as well as a fear of rejection. In all of my fear, I could never have known, that ultimately I had been taught to abandon and reject my—self.

My Life-The Matrix

"**Y**OU'RE SICK LISA YOU know that? Look at what you're doing to the kids. I called your mother you know. She said she thinks you have a hormonal problem or something and that's why you want a divorce," Steven said.

Feeling judged by others had become like a mole on my skin. I didn't necessarily like it, but I learned to accept that it would always be there. As if a spotlight from the cosmos was destined to dance on my back, feeling singled out had become a sad norm.

Steven knew how I felt about my relationship with my mother. Many times in the past I had tried to explain how criticized and judged I felt by her. It crippled me deeply whenever Steven chose to use my pus to his advantage. Like petroleum jelly you might use on a tight fitting pipe, Steven rubbed me down with the fear of my mothers' judgments whenever I refused to budge.

When I was small, it was common for my parents to watch television shows with my brother, sister and me. Marc, Leslie and I would lie on the carpet in front of the television, while my parents sat on the sofa couch behind us. My heart would pick up speed as the shows came to an end. Good night kisses were customary in our home, and the shows end meant it was time for bed.

"Oh my God! Lisa you kiss like a dead fish," my mother said, more than once, and more times than the lonely little girl in me cared to remember.

"Jesus, you're lips are so hard," she'd say, pushing me away, as she wiped her smiling lips off with the back of one of her hands, pretending her remark was not the knife she intended to be. I'd wonder what her comments meant, while I simultaneously wished she just wouldn't say anything at all.

My sister and I shared a bed in a room. A wooden banister lined the staircase that lead to the place where we slept. I recall clinging to it. It was the safe place, the middle ground between the people I loved, and my room. It was there, with my tiny hand placed firmly on the first knotted post of the wooden rail, that I would find the courage to say "Goodnight mommy and daddy. I love you."

I remember the needing I felt within the cells of my being. So starved for the words my heart and mind needed to hear, I knew that unless I said "I love you," I'd never hear those quenching words fall from their lips. But all too often, the blasé' pitch in their voice and the trail in their words, let me know their sentiments were thin. The needing was all in my head.

It was mind thrashing to comprehend that the man that I married delighted in dousing my already charred heart with gasoline, and was all too willing to set it ablaze when I stepped out of line, or beat out of his tune. It was getting harder not to hate him. My patience and empathy for him lessened, as the being in me was finding the courage to feel.

"Can you see the similarities Lisa? Can you see that you are still very much that little girl you were when you were ten? You still chase love? You still try to take care of others so that they eventually take care of you. Your husband stirs within you very similar feelings as the ones you felt for your mother when you were younger. Would you agree?" Ed asked.

"Yes I would. Oh my God Ed! I can't believe it," I said to my therapist, at one of the most memorable of our Tuesday afternoon therapy sessions. "I married my mother."

It's Okay To
Look Now

I T WAS TUESDAY. I was glad. My therapy session with Ed would begin at 12:45 in the afternoon, and it would end just in time for me to get Niccole from pre-k.

"How do you feel today?" Ed, asked as I sat across from him in the broom closet of an office, where we met each week.

"I feel very angry lately and I am not sure why," I said.

"Hmm…really? Is that a problem?" he asked, confusing me.

"I don't understand? What do you mean 'Is this a problem?' Of course it is. I don't want to feel this way," I continued, as Ed scribbled on his long yellow tablet. I didn't like it when he did that. I always wondered what he was jotting down. I knew I was supposed to be learning not to worry or obsess or attach myself to what others thought about me, but Ed was my therapist. And quite honestly, I could not-not care about what he thought about me.

"When you were a child, did you feel as if your brother and sister were encouraged to express emotions like anger?" Ed questioned.

"No. No. No. Are you kidding? We were not allowed to show our feelings at all. We weren't allowed to cry, or shout, or even tell our parents about what we were upset about. Shit, we weren't even allowed to be upset," I said, almost laughing through my teeth. His question seemed absurd. And by the placid expression on Ed's face, I knew that my answer really wasn't the least bit funny. Noticing him, notice my less than appropriate response to what proved to be a deeply ingrained rotten seed in what was the soil of my belief systems, made me feel like there were ants in my pants.

"How about your parents? Did they express their anger?" Ed asked, prodding me to dig deeper for more puzzle pieces.

"Yes. My mother was angry a lot, and a matter of fact, most of the time," I answered.

"How did you know she was angry? How did she express her anger?"

"When my mother was angry she would rant, and rave and sing her long lists of complaints about me, or my sister or my brother, while she was banging cabinet doors, or yanking the long hose of her vacuum around the house. If she was really mad, she'd clench her teeth, and get in our faces, and yell until her face turned cherry red," I answered, not smiling now.

"Did she hit you when she got angry?"

"Yes, sometimes." I said.

"Did she curse you?" Ed continued prodding.

"Yes," I said, digging deeper.

"Did she ever label you as bad, or selfish, or call you any other mean names?" Ed didn't stop.

"Yes. She said I was bad a lot. She called me selfish all the time. She said I'd never have any friends. She called me a hermit. She'd embarrass me in front of others, and make me feel exposed. She was sarcastic. She said no one would ever want to be my friend. She called me a liar. She said I was too sensitive. She said I was over emotional. She said I wasn't nice. She said one day I'd end up like my Aunt Evelyn," I replied, forcing myself to keep the connections to my childhood memories flowing.

"And who is Aunt Evelyn?"

"She is my father's sister. When I was about ten years old or so, she was diagnosed with Paranoid Schizophrenia."

"I know why you're angry now," Ed said, as he handed me a soft, white tissue for the pain filled canoes that began to seep from the edges of my eyes.

"Lisa, depression is anger that has been suppressed. Depression is anger that has been turned inward. You are angry now, because for the first time in your life you are taking *you* seriously. By journaling, you are finally allowing the child in you to feel all the emotions you were once conditioned to believe you had no right to feel, including anger. Sometimes, when a person is severely codependent, they lose the ability to distinguish between emotions, and very often the only emotion they can connect to are negative emotions. My hunch is there is an array of emotions you may be experiencing right now, but at this point in time the one sentiment you can distinguish is anger. Can you feel anything right now besides anger?" he asked.

" I feel sad. I feel lost. I feel confused. I feel like I was treated unfairly. I feel like my mother took her anger out on me. I feel beat up. I feel invisible. I feel exposed. I feel bullied. I feel ignored. I feel abused. I feel abandoned. I feel ashamed. I feel guilty. I feel manipulated. I feel used. I feel unimportant, invalid, and shafted too. I didn't deserve this. It wasn't my responsibility to understand my mother or my father. It was their responsibility to understand me. And they didn't. They never considered my feelings, ever. And that pisses me off, because for as long as I can remember, all I have ever done was worry about other peoples feelings," I said, noticing s sense of relief coming over me.

"As you continue to think about you, and as you continue to learn to *allow* yourself to feel *all* the emotions your parents conditioned you to believe you were not entitled to feel, your appreciation for self will grow. Right now it is very important that you understand how to cope with anger. You do *not* have to *react* to it. But, you do have to learn how to give yourself permission to experience it. And once you have integrated the emotion, you can then let it go. Once you learn to let the anger go, it will no longer be able to keep you stuck," he explained.

Ed was right, like he had been about everything else. I was stuck. But now at least I knew why.

"Do you think I will ever get better Ed, I mean really better?" I asked, seriously wondering if a complete recovery from codependency was possible, aware that what was wrong, was the very foundation that made me--me.

"Lisa, you can not heal, what you do not allow yourself to feel," was his candid and eloquent response. "The more you feel, the deeper you heal, and the better you deal," he continued, flashing me a reassuring grin.

Needing-Wanting-Shame

I VERY RARELY SPENT MONEY on myself. It's not like Steven and I didn't have money to spend, and it's not like Steven ever made me feel like I shouldn't spend money on myself. I just never did. Although my children always had the latest gadget or two, and although I made sure to buy Steven the things that he said he wanted, I only spent money on myself when it was completely necessary. Money and me were like vinegar and bees.

I was scolded for wanting when I was a child. Being called selfish was routine in our home. I was told to be happy for what I had. I was told money didn't grow on trees, and that it wasn't polite to ask for things. I was told that I should be happy I had a roof over my head, and clothes on my back. I was told it was bad to covet, and to envy children who had the things that I didn't. And perhaps worse than being labeled selfish, I was made to believe I didn't deserve anything.

Feeling undeserving ran deep within me, and deeper than I consciously realized. When Steven moved out he took ownership over our financial affairs. I didn't feel I had the right to insist he not take our checkbooks with him when he left. Guilt for wanting to end our marriage had surely hindered my ability to speak up for myself. With Steven out of the house now, I was at his mercy when it came to money.

So accustomed to having emotions pull me around by my nose, I failed to see then what I see now. Deeply ingrained within a groove in my mind was the belief that I was selfish. At the time, this sinking belief poisoned me more than I ever could have known. On the cusp of self-awareness, I was beginning to see how diseased my self-image had sadly become, and how necessary it was going to be to overcome this negative sense, if I were ever going to be able to fight for what was rightfully mine.

My refrigerator, freezer and cupboards were nearly bare before I approached Steven about needing money to buy groceries for the kids and I. My body trembled the first time I approached Steven for money to buy groceries as well as for a new vacuum cleaner. The vacuum cleaner I had been using died not long after Steven left. I was terrified to tell him we needed a new one. Steven had me right where he wanted me. I needed him now and we both knew it.

Steven could read my emotions in a scholarly way. He understood how to play my wounds to his gain, and especially enjoyed using my mother's chronic negative opinion of me to his advantage. Streetwise, Steven played the selfish card whenever I approached him for money. And as if I were ten and in want of a pair of authentic Ked's, my veins would swim in shame for needing at all.

.

Breaking Me Means Breaking Them— Why Can't You See?

WHEN I FINALLY FOUND the courage to ask Steven for money, he snickered through the sucking of food out of his teeth, and said, "I ain't giving you shit. Use your credit cards. My lawyer wants to track what you spend anyway," he continued. He was standing in front of his mother's house. She was stationed off to the side of her front door. Her elbow was still visible, although I assumed she didn't know that it was. Unlike me, Steven knew his mother had his back..

"This is divorce Lisa. You wanna keep going to therapy, and keep talking to lawyers, then this is the way it is going to be," he said, as he leaned over my son and in through the passenger side window of our minivan. My two younger daughters were in the backseats.

"Steven, are you saying it's okay to use my credit cards?" I asked him, wishing to be clear. My only concern was that I was going to be able to buy groceries for my children. I didn't give a rats' ass about his lawyer wanting to track what I spent. I knew Steven was only trying to push me around anyway. Because Steven was usually passive aggressive, and most times it was impossible to get him to answer a question with a direct answer, my objective was a simple one.

"Yea yea sure. Use the cards. It's fine. You don't think I am going to give you cash do you?" he continued almost laughing as he spoke.

I drove away from the curb thankful that Steven and I had been able to have somewhat of a decent conversation about money. I was grateful my children were spared another discomforting episode between their mother and father. Relieved, I drove the kids to Target and told them they could each buy something special for themselves, hoping to give them something to look forward to.

The kids and I took our time shopping that day. It had been a long time since we had purchased anything, including food. After Steven moved out and money got scarce, the kids and I started taking advantage of the New York City Libraries. No longer able to take my children to every new movie that debut, I began to get them used to borrowing video's and books from the library. Applebee's and sushi, were replaced with home cooked pasta and vegetable meals. No longer able to buy the latest video games, we learned to fly kites and played Frisbee instead. Although the kids and I were doing our best to enjoy the lemonade we were making with our lemons, I knew the sudden contrasts in their life experiences were still bitter pills for them to swallow.

My shopping cart was full to the brim with everything from cereal to shampoo. Amongst our much-needed groceries was a football for Max, a paint set for Amanda, and a stuffed dog for Niccole. For the first time in a long time my children seemed relaxed and almost happy. This shopping spree of sorts did all of us good.

The store was unusually busy for nine o'clock in the morning. Niccole was especially bubbly as we approached the cashier and Max and I began emptying the contents of our cart onto the black conveyor belt. Unconcerned with the totals that were being tallied, I focused in on how at ease my children seemed, and nestled into appreciating a moment I once considered a chore.

"Cash or credit?" the cashier asked. And with that, I handed the overweight young man in tan pants and a red shirt my credit card. When within seconds the chubby face looked me in the eye and said, "Denied," I thought I misunderstood him.

"There must be some kind of a mistake," I said, suggesting he try the card again. When he did and the card was denied a second time, I handed him a second card. When that card was denied, I handed him my third and last card, and prayed with all of me the card would go through.

"Denied again lady—your credits no good," he said.

Back In The Drivers Seat

I F GUILT OR FEAR ever consumed me, these emotions were gone now, as rage lit me up like a matchstick that had been tossed on a gasoline-drenched bundle of dry lumber. Unable to feel guilt or shame through the smog of my burning rage, I instructed the bloated cashier to hold onto my cart.

"I'll be back," I said firmly.

Dripping with disdain for Steven and his little games, I darted my children into the parking lot, and hurried them into our car.

"Don't you guys worry, mommy is going to make sure everything is okay," I told my kids, hoping to ease their anxieties. It was difficult for me to feel anything besides rage for their father now. Used to bearing the brunt of Steven's ignorance, I was unaccustomed to not being able to deflect my children from this sort of pain. Steven had gone too far this time, and all I wanted now was to make this wrong right, and as soon as possible.

Steven was standing where I left him. A devilish smile swept across his face as I zipped my van in front of where he stood. My belly flopped when I noticed the smirk he shared with one of his short brothers.

"Yeah what do you want now Lisa?" Steven said, as I jumped out of my seat, slammed the car door, and approached him face to face.

Steven towered over me, and I didn't care.

"Do you think this shit is funny? Do you think that telling me to use credit cards that you knew would be denied to buy our children food is funny? Do you think that humiliating our children publicly in a town they live in is funny? Do you think that by suffocating me with money that--that is going to, in someway make me cave in and come back to you? Do you think that I would want a man that could do that to his children? Do you even realize how cruel you are?" I ranted at Steven, who stood there silently, his face no longer wearing a grin.

"I have a cart full of groceries waiting for me back at the store. I need three hundred dollars to go buy them, and you're going to give it to me right now. And don't you ever, ever pull shit like that with me again," I demanded, from a place within me I didn't know I had.

As Steven stroked one hundred dollar bills out from the pocket of his dirty pants, "You should be ashamed of yourself," I said.

"Alright--alright calm down you lunatic. Here go buy the kids food. And hey, don't spend any of my money on you—ya' hear me?" the father of my children yelled as I turned from him and walked away.

The Pink Elephants Are Coming

I T WAS MY BIRTHDAY. My mother called to tell me she wanted Steven and I to bring the kids by to have pizza and cake for me at her house. I was tired. My mind felt like it had been running a marathon for weeks. I was too weak to argue, and too drained to explain to her why Steven had no reason to be there. Still in the very early stages of our separation, he and I had yet to legalize an agreement between us. My parents, I believed were hoping we'd find someway to reconcile.

I was struggling greatly with guilt. Max cried often, while Amanda seemed to hold her feelings in. My baby Niccole spoke less frequently, and when she did, she spoke only to me. Her pacifier became something we learned we could never leave home without. I was aware at how differently my children were experiencing as well as expressing their feelings. And it was all I could do not to feel toppled over by the grief this awareness was sweeping up inside of me. I agreed to ask Steven to come along.

It was pizza and Carvel cake served on paper plates, and coffee for six adults, served in ceramic mugs. My brother's wife was at the sink, putting the finishing touches on the mugs. My children, Steven and I were gathered at the dining room table surrounded by the rest of my family.

I felt like a zit. All eyes on me, I was aware that my every move was being monitored. Afraid to say the wrong thing that could possibly trigger an attack, I said what I thought was general and safe.

"I am so tired today," I said as I brushed hair out of my face.

My mother was standing behind me and leaning against a wall.

"Tired? How could you be tired? You didn't lift a friggin' finger the whole time you've been here," she said, as Steven smiled an approving grin her way.

Earlier that day I had had a therapy session with Ed.

"The next time you feel verbally assaulted, instead of denying how it makes you feel, stop in that moment and ask yourself how it feels. Sit with the feelings that stir up inside of you, and really allow yourself to feel them," he had suggested during the session earlier.

I sat for a moment and allowed what my mother had said to sink in. It wasn't just what she said. It wasn't just the way she said it. It was much deeper than that, and she and everyone at that table knew it, although like the pink elephants that had littered our lives, no one dared confront the stench. Instead, like when I was a child, I was expected to ignore the picking of my scabs, and pretend her comments were not the assaults we all knew they were.

As usual, my father said nothing when my mother took her emotional swing. So accustomed to ignoring the verbal grenades my mother often launched, my family sat and waited until the sting of the attack slithered under the dining room rug. Compounding my grief now, was the idea that my mother was in many ways kicking me when I was down, and to the benefit of my soon to be ex-husband.

As sadness washed over me like a wave on a shore, my being began to collapse under the weight of what I could no longer ignore. Tears were forming in my eyes, when I stood up from the table and walked into a rear room. I wanted to leave and was now searching for all of my children's coats when my sister entered the room and noticed me crying.

"Don't leave Lisa," Leslie said, as I struggled not to let all of my tears flow.

Just then my children began to enter the room where Leslie and I stood.

"Mommy, why are you crying?" Amanda asked, as my trembling fingers slipped her winter coat over her shoulders. For a moment I considered lying and covering up for her grandmother. But then I realized that would be wrong. My child was sensing something that was real, and she deserved for her feelings to be validated.

"I am crying because grandma is being mean to me, and I don't like how that feels," I said. "So we're going home."

My children were all bundled up and ready to go when my mother appeared in the doorway of the rear room.

"Where you going?" my mother asked; a dish towel over her shoulder, and one of her hands on her hip.

"I am not twelve anymore! You don't have the right to push me around! I don't have to feel like a little girl around you, and you don't have the right to embarrass me in front of my children! If you can't speak to me like the adult I am or in the way I deserve to be spoken to, then stay out of my life. You enjoy embarrassing me in front of Steven and my children? Oh my God Ma! Don't you see how much I need a mother right now? What's wrong with you?" I said, as my body shook almost convulsively. Stunned, my mother did not say a word. No one did.

"Come on kids lets go home," I said.

This Isn't About Me Anymore

ARC MET MY CHILDREN and I in the hallway between the kitchen and the back room. He looked angry, and his voice was stern when he shouted,

"You know what Lee, if you're that pissed off, get the hell out of here, and go home."

I wasn't surprised by Marc's visceral reaction, or by my father's. My father was sitting at the head of the dining room table with his hands pressed firmly against his ears. He was shaking his head from side to side.

"You cause nothing but problems Lisa, go home. You wanna make a big deal outta this shit, then go ahead, go on and go," Marc continued, angry that I had upset his mother and caused such a fuss.

It was out in the open now. Whatever the muck was that stood between my family and I, had been splattered all over my mother and father's mint green living room. Nothing had really changed since I was seven or ten. Marc and my mother were still the tag team they had always been, my father was still playing the role of the family ostrich, and like Switzerland Leslie preferred the neutral zones.

I left my family's house that evening full of grief. As if all the pain I had ever ignored was rising to the surface in one giant shot, I found myself wondering how it was I was ever going to find the strength to keep moving ahead. Although I was aware that my family was a codependent dynamic unit that operated under the veils of denial, and that as I recovered from codependency in my personal life, I would inevitably need to confront my familial dysfunction in the process, I was not prepared for the enormous fortitude it would require to do so, or the avalanches of grief that were becoming as familiar as breath itself.

Why Me?

A T MY NEXT THERAPY session with Ed I told him about the showdown that had occurred between my mother, brother and I at my birthday dinner. The emotional explosion didn't surprise Ed.

"Very often when codependents begin to get well, their families don't appreciate the accountability the codependents begin to dish out," he explained.

"All I did was act like I was disrespected and humiliated. All I did was appropriately respond to what my mother said, and everyone got angry with me for doing so. My reaction was truthful. Her words hurt, and they were unnecessary. And the fact that she said what she said in front of Steven only made my personal matters with him worse. I think if she has a right to say what she feels, then I have a right to respond to how what she says makes me feel," I said.

"Lisa, you're beginning to understand that you have the right to be treated fairly by others. While that is a good thing, you must also be aware that others have the right to treat you unfairly," Ed continued, making sure to help me continue to think deeper.

"Yeah that's fine," I said, "but I don't have to tolerate being treated unfairly, and I am beginning to understand that now. My family doesn't see me Ed. And it's about time I learn to accept that, and stop hoping that one day that will change. I can't worry about trying to please them anymore. I have to learn to somehow let them go out of love, and not out of anger. I have to learn how to love without expectation, in spite of all the expectations I know my family has of me."

I wasn't sure what was going to happen next between my family and I. In my childhood home we didn't know how to communicate effectively or how to respect the feelings of one another. If my parents had something to say, they just said it, and it didn't seem to matter if what they said caused us emotional harm. Criticism, judgments, sarcasm, and glares were commonplace. And if one of my siblings or I ever dared to have an open emotional reaction to a negative comment that was tossed our way, we were then chastised for having any feelings at all. Life was lived on eggshells, and broken glass.

With my marriage gasping its last breaths, my emotional skin was raw. In all fairness to the people in my life at that time, it would not have taken much to push my mind over the edge. I was too vulnerable and too empty at the time to be able to hold back the emotions I for so long had stuffed inside. No longer able to worry what might happen next after I confronted my mother, I felt forced to let the cards fall where they might. Too tired to care what might happen next, I rolled with the motions of my emotions and let go, faintly aware that I was taking my codependent recovery on the road.

If I were ever going to heal, I had to first learn how to give myself permission to feel what others had always insisted I had no right to experience. The consequences of my newfound understandings however, made my mind feel like it was caught in a boats propeller. Confronting my mother meant I had to confront all the emotions I had locked away since I was a small child. Understanding on an intellectual level however, that the turmoil of the present moment was necessary for my desired future recovery, helped me value the experiences of the moment rather than collapse under them.

Same Game-
New Rules

S TEVEN WATCHED THE KIDS so I could go. The Al-Anon meeting was over by nine. It was nine fifteen. The kids and their father were all sitting on our maroon leather couch. Steven stood up when I walked into the kitchen. "Thanks for watching the kids tonight. I appreciate it," I said.

"How was your AA meeting?" he asked loudly so our children could hear.

"I didn't go to an AA meeting. I went to an Al-Anon meeting."

"It's the same shit," he said.

"No, its not. Al-Anon is for codependents." "Whatever. So did it help you get your head screwed on straight?" he asked, getting closer to me now. I didn't answer.

"So uh, why are you going to meetings for alcoholics? You're not an alcoholic," Steven asked.

"The meeting is for people who are struggling with issues like codependency," I replied. "Lisa, you're not an alcoholic, and neither am I. What's wrong with you? You're taking this shit too far," he said.

"Thanks for watching the kids tonight. I am tired and I am sure the kids are too," I said, hoping Steven would leave.

I was grateful I had taken another step. Determined to one day be completely self reliant, required that I be willing to think new thoughts and take new risks. So conditioned to living inside a box, attending an Al Anon meeting felt like I had jumped out of a plane. It wasn't okay to take risks in my family. It wasn't okay to think thoughts that the people that I loved could not understand. Something that should have been as simple as going to a meeting that I thought might support me in some way made me a target for criticism, judgments and emotional punishment.

I wished I could talk to Steven about my meetings without him rolling his eyes, or making tiny circles with his pointer finger near the side of his head--the hand signal that implied I was loopy. A huge part of me pitied him because I knew he'd never change. A part of me struggled with guilt over the fact that I was going to leave the man I married behind. I had to. He left me no other choice.

As my understanding of codependency deepened, so much of what was wrong in my life became clear. Years of begging Steven to embark on a journey towards emotional health together had come to a tragic end. It was time to learn how to let go.

"Thanks again for watching the kids," I said, urging Steven to leave.

"Yeah sure, whatever Lisa. They're my kids right? And I should be the one watching them while you go to your AA meetings right?" Steven replied, wishing to bait me into an argument.

"I am not sure when my next Al Anon meeting will be. But I will let you know," I said, ushering him out the front door.

"Come on kids. It's time for mama to put you three little rugrats to bed," I said, turning towards my children, and certain to flash them a smile that told them their mommy was alright.

The Dotted Line

I ONLY TOLD ROSEY. I was thankful for our friendship, and grateful my children trusted her.

My knees knocked the entire ride.

"Hello Mrs. Romano, please have a seat." She was a short woman with blonde hair I assumed she got out of a bottle. She was slightly on the heavy side, and her fashion style was causal but chic. Her office was neat but in a messy sort of way. She didn't fit my assumption of what a divorce attorney would look like. And quite frankly I didn't care.

As if my body was being pushed forward by a source I could not name, I often wondered where I was deriving the strength to endure the never-ending twists and turns my journey had become.

"You look anxious. Are you feeling alright?" my divorce attorney asked.

"I am anxious actually. This is all so surreal to me," I said, shivering from the adrenaline that had caused my blood vessels to constrict.

"Are your parents alive?" my attorney asked.

"Yes," I said.

"Would you like me to call them? We could wait until they arrived. Perhaps you'd feel less anxious if they were here with you."

"No thank you. That won't be necessary," I said, as I nervously tore her retainer fee from my blue checkbook sleeve.

Not long after I confronted Steven about our overdue credit cards, he told me he was going to allow me to continue paying our house bills.

"Just don't buy yourself anything with my money," he instructed.

So alone on unknown terrain, it took a titanic effort not to slip into an emotional abyss. This next move would turn my world upside down. The pink elephants in my life would have to find someplace else to roam. The insides of me would now be in black and white. Everything that I had ever known was coming to an end. I sensed in my gut something more powerful than fear was with me now. I couldn't taste it or touch it, but I could perceive that it was there. As if I suddenly had not one spirit but two, support had shown up, and just in the knick of time.

Perhaps it was awareness that had been born of truth, or maybe the lightening of my load that helped me stay strong that day. I wasn't sure what to call this newfound clarity I now had. A book that I had been reading spoke of the higher self. I wondered if that was what I was sensing in my new unclouded perceptions. Whatever it was, I knew it was there. On the afternoon that I signed my old life away in black and white, I was grateful not only for Rosey, but for this higher power too.

Months before Steven had moved out, I had pleaded with him to join me in therapy. My feelings for my husband had begun to wane. And when for the first time in my marriage I began to notice men notice me, I was certain more trouble than I desired might be on the way. I told Steven my feelings for him were changing. I told him too, that I was beginning to feel a pull for the attraction of other men. I hoped with all of my being that my confession would spark within him a desire to put effort into our dissolving relationship.

Steven was wearing light blue cotton shorts, and a white t-shirt. He was standing near the fridge and had a gallon of milk in his hand. I was seated at our Formica kitchen table, when I unbuttoned my heart. It was early in the morning, and the kids were still asleep.

"Steven I want to feel attracted to you and only you. I don't want to be in a relationship with anyone else but you. I don't want our marriage to end. That's why I am trying so hard to fix whatever might be wrong with us. If you told me you were feeling pulled out of our marriage by another woman, oh my God, that would kill me. I would do anything I could to get you to feel that way about me. Don't you care how I feel about you? Don't you ever worry how I see you?" I pleaded with him, that early morning, hoping that what I had so openly revealed would provoke a desire in him to heal our union.

"Honestly Lisa, I never think about how you feel. Nope, I never think about how you feel about me," he said nonchalantly, as he placed the gallon of milk back into the fridge.

Steven's remote admission felt like he had yanked my heart out of my chest. One of the heaviest straws of our marriage thus far, his aloof response to my heartfelt admission caused a deep gash in whatever hope I was clinging to about us. I wanted to hold onto our marriage, but after Steven confessed that he never considered my feelings, I realized there was no—us. There was just me—and my illusions that had me blinded. I didn't love what we were. I had been in love with what I wished we could be.

"Sign right here Mrs. Romano," my attorney said, pointing to a bold X on a sheet of heavy stock paper; my signature, in many ways marking the beginning of the end. And as my heart thumped ferociously like wild horses running all about on the inside of my upper body, it was the image of Steven standing in front of our fridge wearing his light blue shorts, that filled my head in those moments, as I signed my name on the dotted line that pivotal unforgettable day.

Flower Child

"OW ARE YOU SURVIVING financially these days Lisa?" Ed asked. It was Tuesday, and I was relieved.

"Well, I have had to cut back on many of the things the kids and I were used to. I don't drive unless I have to, because I want to save money on gas, and I no longer order food from restaurants, or buy fast food. I cook every night to save money. I have also stopped taking the kids to the movies, and we don't go bowling anymore either. I took them to the library and got them library cards. I never realized it before, but you can rent video's there for free, and they offer all kinds of programs for children too," I said.

"How do you feel about these new changes?" he asked inquisitively.

"Once I got over the initial jolt of reality, and I came to accept that Steven was not going to make things easy for me financially, my mind started to come up with solutions to address my concerns about money. When I actually broke my budget down, I realized there was a whole lot of excess spending that was truly unnecessary," I explained confidently.

"So you made a list of wants –vs-needs?"

"I suppose I did," I answered, giggling a little.

"You will not die when you move out of your house, nor will your children. You will not die from having to get a job, or from eating pasta for dinner five nights out of the week. And you will not die if nobody you love understands, or approves of your decisions about your life. You may want them to validate you, but you do not need them to in order to survive this life," Ed remarked, helping me keep ever clearly connected to my growing ability to make choices rather than resort to feeling like a victim.

"I noticed something interesting about flowers the other day," I began to share with Ed, "I noticed that they instinctively lean towards the sun," I said.

"Yes, and your point is what Lisa?" Ed asked sounding slightly amused.

"I found it interesting that flowers, and trees all embrace growth. They all seem to lean in the direction of what feels right. I admire that," I said to my half-smiling therapist Ed.

"I sense there is more you'd like to say," he replied.

"Well, I think that is the way it should be for all living things, and I am guessing that is the way it was intended to be--this universe of ours. Humans are supposed to be the superior race. Yet we aren't as smart as daffodils. I never leaned towards the sun. Instead I craved the dark. And that makes me sort of sad. Do you think I would have been a happy little flower of a girl if my parents weren't adult children of alcoholics?" I asked Ed, curious about what he thought about my insights.

"I think you were robbed. But I think your parents were too," he said.

Ed was right. It wasn't my parent's fault. Although neither of my parents ever took the time to understand how their parent's alcoholism had affected them, they somehow managed to be better parents than their own. As my understandings of codependency and the affects of alcoholism on a family dynamic expanded, so did my appreciation for my parents, in spite of all the mistakes they had made. My parents, like me—were victims of unconscious and dysfunctional belief systems, and it was making less and less sense to blame them for issues they weren't even aware that they had.

The Shower Scene

IT FELT LIKE I had been trapped inside a scene from a horror movie, only that the camera was in my head.

It was a Saturday morning. The kids were still in bed and I was taking a shower. While tilting my head back to rinse shampoo from my hair, a sudden feeling of ick came upon me. Unnerved, and unsure why I felt so disturbed, I opened my eyes. Adrenaline shot through my veins like ice water when I noticed the silhouette of a large man standing in the threshold that lead to my bathroom. Sudden fright pulled me to my knees. Terror slammed my hands against the wet walls of my shower, as my body slid against the slick glass enclosure and my naked body crumpled to the sudsy floor below.

My eyes burning from shampoo, I let out a scream and decayed into a ball. Unconsciously hoping that the shadowy silhouette in my doorway belonged to Steven, it was moments before my mind was able to grab hold of its self long enough to open my eyes to see if the dark figure was still standing there. When my eyes did open and I found no shadow there, for a split second I wondered if I were going insane.

In my gut I knew Steven was fucking with my head. But like children prancing about on a trampoline, feelings like doubt, dismay, confusion, and terror bounced about in my consciousness regardless. Amidst the ricochet of emotions, I could hear my mind wonder if Steven was smarter than I thought he was. Was he deliberately trying to drive me over the edge, or were his antics much like knee jerk reactions to his unwelcomed sense of powerlessness?

Trembling ferociously I wrapped my body in a towel and made my way to the phone that was resting on my side of the bed. Before reaching for the phone, I made sure to first re-lock my bedroom door. Clinging for a sense of sanctity now, I called my brother Marc hoping that because he was a police officer, and because in my opinion Steven had threatened my person, he would be able to not only calm me, but talk some sense into my mind fucking husband.

Clinging to my last threads, I had grown weary from Steven's recent games. In the weeks that had lead up to this point in time, he had threatened to take my children to Canada. He said he would kidnap them and live there with his family and that there would be nothing I could do about it. He also said that his family knew a number of judges in the court system and that there was no way I was ever going to win custody. He and his family routinely made aggressive remarks whenever they saw me out in public, as well as flashed me hate filled glares. When Steven did put money in the bank accounts or dropped cash off by our house, he always interrogated me in front of my children first. Once he even told my son to take me home and to smack some sense into me, after he and I got into one of our routine spats.

It was odd for me to reach out to Marc. He and I had never had a comfortable relationship. And although I understood the root causes why, I never completely lost hope that one day we'd feel truly like kin. I was desperate now, and needed my brother to hear me and to protect me too. Beyond able to be concerned for what Marc would think of me reaching out to him, desperation prompted me to make the call and to hope for the best.

"Marc it's me. I don't know what to do. Steven just broke into my room and he was standing in the doorway of the bathroom just standing there looking at me naked," I said crying through each word.

"Lee, Lee, calm the hell down. I can hardly understand what you are saying," Marc said.

"I was taking a shower. My doors were closed, and Steven came home and opened my bathroom door. It was locked. At least I think it was locked. Steven was standing there. Just staring at me. He didn't say a word. He was just standing there staring at me as I was taking a shower. I didn't know he was there. I was washing my hair. He scared me so bad. My heart is beating so fast. I can't stop shaking. I don't know what to do. I screamed and he left. I am not sure if he's still in the house. Oh my God what if he does something else? What if this just keeps getting worse? I can't take much more of this Marc. He is trying to drive me insane. I know it. I just know it. He does all this sneaky shit behind people's backs. I know I sound nuts. But I am not. This shit is really happening Marc. It's really happening," I begged Marc to listen.

"What? You're upset because Steven snuck a peak at you while you were in the shower? Steven is your husband. What's the big deal if he took a peek at you while you were naked? He's still your husband ya' know. And by the way—that's still his house too," my brother the police officer said.

Got A Match?

MY MENTAL EQUILIBRIUM WAS off. Dazed by the sound of the bell, I hesitantly opened the door.

"So uh, how ya' doin' Lee?" my brother asked. I didn't know what to say. As if there were huge holes in me now, my mind felt fussy and was slow to root out words to articulate the insecure disorientation that seemed to have kidnapped my soul. For the life of me, I couldn't make heads or tails out of Marc's lack of empathy for the position I was in. I couldn't help but doubt my sanity.

Oddly, I felt myself aware at how arduous of an attempt I had been making to hold myself together in front of my brother. Beneath my skins surface was an intense need not to appear weak. But as I noticed him, notice peculiarity in me, my souls load burst forth like a wave. Against my minds will, emotions spurt forth beyond my control.

"Lisa what the hell is wrong with you?" my brother said, as my muscles began to tremble, and my eyes began to cry.

"You better pull yourself together girl. You remind me of some of the domestically abused housewives I have had to deal with as a police officer. Geez…relax," he said.

Marc couldn't see me, in fact he never could. Our sibling bond had been eaten away decades before. It was not his fault, nor was it mine.

It was like moving a mountain to reach out for help, and especially to reach out to Marc. I explained as plainly as I could that I was afraid of what Steven might be capable of next. I told my brother that Steven's aggression was only getting worse.

Marc told me there wasn't much he could do. Because he was a New York City Police Officer, he had to be careful how he approached Steven. Marc promised me he'd at least talk to Steven, and ask him not to break into my bedroom or to invade my private space. It wasn't my wish list, but I was grateful regardless. Steven was a bully who liked to do his work in the dark. I hoped that once Steven realized I was reaching out to my family in spite of how I knew they perceived me that maybe he'd back off.

A few hours later, my phone rang. It was Marc. He told me that he had called Steven. He said Steven asked him out to lunch. He said they shared a couple of beers. He said he asked Steven to back off and to not break into my bedroom anymore, and also told him it was best if he called before he wanted to come by to see the kids. I remember the heavy feeling I felt in my chest, as my brother recanted his afternoon with Steven. Like a snake charmer Steven was playing my brothers tune, and like a Cobra, Marc was under his spell.

My heart continued to sink as Marc went on, but when he said--

"Lisa I gotta' ask you somethin'. Did you really tell Steven that daddy molested you when you were a little girl?"--the Molotov cocktail of a lie Steven had concocted to serve as a diversion to help him escape accountability from my brother, nearly extinguished my soul.

It Only Takes One Little Thought To Turn Things Around

THE LAST BITS OF my world had been yanked from beneath me. The sound of conjecture in my brother's voice flung my spirit to the ground. As if air were glass, every breath hurt. Marc was my last hope. Words lost, my mind went blank. Feeling disoriented, my body lost its ability to stand upright, and slithered to the black and white tile floor in my kitchen. Desperate, I considered reaching out to my therapist Ed, but wondered what would I say? How could I describe the deluge I was experiencing, and to what would I assess the blame? There were no visible signs of the battery I felt. My eyes were not black, and my arms were not bruised. To the world, and just as Steven had hoped, I seemed mentally unfit.

Adrift within the oblivion Steven's fabrication created, I felt lost, dazed, confused and overwhelmed by fear. I could hear my mind wonder if I had been cracked too deeply. Would I be able to survive this lie? Would my parents believe me, or would they believe Steven? Would my father be able to see past the wound Steven's trickery caused, or would he cast me away and blame me for the pain?

Overcome by a battery of emotions, I felt as if I were slipping into an abyss. As tears flowed out of me like rain, my body surrendered to a sacrificial like heartbreak. Weeping to the point of physical exhaustion, my body drifted off to sleep beneath the kitchen sink. I was still groggy when I began to wake up, and I wasn't sure if I was dreaming when from within my own mind I heard a voice say,

"You know you didn't say those things about your father, and I know you didn't say those things about your father, and that's all that matters."

Ed had promised that one day my negative self talk would shift and I would begin having more positive self talk in my head. I wondered if this was the beginning of that shift in my inner dialogue. I wondered if the voice I heard was Ed's? Was it God's voice? Was it my higher power?

As the dreamy state slowly faded into consciousness, I questioned my own sanity. Feeling psychologically fragile, I was easy about bringing myself to my feet. My children were due back soon, and I would need to somehow reduce the swelling of my eyes before they arrived. They were looking forward to spaghetti for dinner, and a mommy with a smile.

I Am Woman

OR A FEW DAYS after his meeting with Marc, Steven didn't bother coming into our house. I was grateful for the reprieve, and took his avoidance as a small sign of an admission of guilt. I didn't care. I couldn't care. I was too busy sewing my soul back together again.

Mother's day was near. When my mother called to ask me what Steven and the kids and I were doing for Mother's day, I told her plainly, there was no 'Steven and I. Steven and I were separated and getting a divorce.' Her silence was tainted with disapproval. Instinctively I knew she understood my position had changed.

Now beyond the ability to cushion my parent's perception of reality, my kids and I showed up at their home without Steven. Riddled with nervousness, I was cautious not to cross any invisible lines when we arrived. Dinner wrapped up without any unsettling remarks. Grateful, I looked forward to coffee and desert and non-combustible superficial conversations with family members around the dining room table.

As small talk began to flow, I felt a growing appreciation for the lighthearted exchanges, and for what felt like a sense of normalcy. Not feeling singled out for being single that day, a secret hope for more of whatever this was—was born in the belly of my soul. Feeling almost free enough to laugh out loud, I prayed my family and I would have more days like these.

Just as my mind began to release its need to stay clutched to fear, Marc decided to tip the topic of conversation my way. Caught off guard when I head him say,

"So uh Lisa, how are you going to survive once you sell your house? And what are you going to do? Are you going to have some other man raise your kids or what? If I were Steven I'd be furious at you. He gave you everything. You went on vacations, lived in a beautiful home, had money in the bank--I mean, geez, I don't think I could put up with losing my wife, my house and my kids. I'd be pissed off at you too. And honestly Lisa, I really could not believe you called me because Steven snuck a peek at you in the shower," Marc mocking me with the tone in his voice, and the patronizing look on his face.

Marc's need to bait me into arguments was nothing new. But unlike so many times before, I was no longer concerned about keeping invisible apple carts steady. The compulsion to censor any reaction to his comments was gone.

Adrenaline shot through my veins like rockets. As my body stiffened, I could feel rage fill my head. So present in the moment, it was not possible for me to conceal the emotions his ordinary insensitivity provoked.

My belly flipped and my head sprung around like someone had smacked it hard when I glared into Marc's eyes and said,

"How dare you! How dare you make remarks about my life! Do you have any idea what it feels like to have your entire life fall apart while the people you love stand by and do nothing but criticize you? Do you have any idea what it's like to go through a divorce with someone who is trying to drive you crazy? Do you have any idea how excruciating it is to watch your children watch you fall apart? Do you have any idea how terrifying it is to *not* know what tomorrow is going to bring? Do you have any concept of how alone I feel, knowing my family has more concern in their hearts for the man who is doing his best to destroy me, than they do for me and my children? Do you have any idea how frightened my children are, and how painful that is for me to know that what I am doing is hurting them, even though I know that what I am doing is right? No you don't Marc. You have no clue, because the truth is you don't give a fucking shit about me, and you never did. But you know what? I am done. I am fucking done with all of you. If you people do not want to support me, while I go through this divorce, then you can stay the fuck out of my life. I am lucky I have the strength to get out of bed in the morning. You see this smile? You see this make-up I put on every morning? What do you think? Do you think because I 'look' okay, that that means I am not in pain? What would you prefer? What would make you be able to accept that I bleed just as much as anyone else? Should I slit my wrists? Should I gain one hundred pounds? Should I overdose on pain-killers? What? What is it going to take for my family to once and for all—fucking validate me and back the fuck off of my case? Tell me! Tell me Marc—when do I begin to matter to all of you—when?"

The Breaking Point

I'D SEEN THAT LOOK in my father's eyes before. I was with my father on the day his sister was diagnosed with paranoid schizophrenia and he was forced to commit her to a mental hospital for treatment. Sitting across from him as I ranted back at Marc, I struggled not to be engulfed by what I believed he must have been feeling. It was grueling enough to hold onto myself, and to hold my own ground. Marc's comment, although paled in comparison to some of the others he had thrown my way in the past, was enough to tear open my thin skin like a dam.

My mother appeared shocked by my uproar. Her mouth quiet, she made herself scarce and removed herself from my field of vision. My sister, her husband and Marc's wife, quickly ushered all of our children out of the next room and escorted them down into my sister's apartment. At the table, there was only Marc, my father and me now.

My body was heaving, and my eyes were weeping. Scarcely below my rage I could sense the rumbling of hate. I hated my family as much as I loved them. I hated that I had been pushed this far. I hated that they had been able to crack me open, and that I was unable to control the sap of my vulnerabilities. Since I was a little girl I had done my best to keep my weaknesses concealed. I was accustomed to wearing armor in their company, and hated that Marc's remark had now stripped me to my core.

Our relationships were hanging in the balance. I was ready to let them all go for the sake of saving my self. My children needed a mother who was going to be strong enough to withstand the storms that were headed their way. A lifetime of surrendering to the dysfunctional family systems I had been born into had taken their toll. Year's prior, when I was playing the denial game in my marriage, and was not being bombarded by the toxic after affects of truth, it was easier to tolerate the dismissive attitudes many of my family members chucked my way. But now, as the consequences of personal truth thundered down on my life like cannons being dropped from the sky, I was in need of identifying more clearly enemy lines.

My children didn't deserve to witness their mother being torn down by the people who presumably should have been supporting her. Concerned not only with the lessons of love my family members were teaching my children, I was just as aware of my desire to teach my children about setting personal boundaries.

As uncomfortable as it was to go toe to toe with the heads of dysfunction in my family, I was assured the stand off was a necessary aspect of my codependent recovery in spite of all the rage and hatred that was rising up in my being.

My father's back was against a wall. As fear consumed him, I could sense his personal struggle. It made me sick to my stomach he struggled at all. He had a choice to make, and the rogue daughter I had become in that moment demanded he make that choice soon. It was getting late, and I had grown weary of this wretched Mother's day.

"It's me or him dad, that's the way it's going to be. Steven is using you against me, and if you won't see it, then I have to let you all go," I said, as my father's gaze seared into my own.

"Lisa, you are scaring me right now, ya know. I don't want to say it, but you are reminding me of you know who," my father said, as he shook his finger my way as well as his head.

For a split moment I was sucked back in time. Like shadows with trumpets I could hear my mother say, that I was going to grow up like Aunt Evelyn, the family paranoid schizophrenic. He didn't want to say it, but he did. Daddy was comparing me to his sister. Here we were, father and daughter, battling it out for my soul. He wanted me to bend. He wanted me to stuff my feelings. He wanted me to smile. He wanted me to disown my self, and to disengage from my rage. He wanted me to be more concerned about what he thought about me, than what I thought about him.

Revelations flashed rapidly across the screens in my mind. Everything that Ed had warned me about was happening. He said my family would try and stuff me back into old patterns. He said the family I loved was going to get angry when I got well. He said denial was as real as air, and just as difficult to see or to grasp. He said I'd eventually have to make a choice between them and me. Ed was right. The more educated I became about the dynamics of codependency, the clearer it was for me to see my family's denial.

"You want me to call Steven? Is that what you want me to do?" my father asked.

My family could not see, that this chaotic and explosive episode had less to do with Steven, than it had to do with who and what our family had always been. Steven was wrong for treating me abusively, and although I did not accept his behavior, I could comprehend his aggression. I was leaving him, and in his mind, I had hurt him. My family however, had no excuse for pushing me around. I'd spent a lifetime trying to convince Marc and Leslie that I was a big sister who loved them, and had only their best interests at heart. And I'd spent just as much time trying to be good enough for parents who still, for their own personal reasons, could not see the worthwhile being I was, who needed only to be validated by the people she loved.

"Daddy, I want you to do what any father would do and protect his daughter from a man who was trying to hurt her. I want you to want to get involved. I want you to at least let Steven know you are aware he's playing mind games with me and with you. Daddy you and mommy invite Steven over for dinner! What message do you think that is sending him? Daddy he uses all of you against me. Don't you understand how hurtful that is to me? Can't you understand how hard this divorce is on me? It's hard enough watching my babies be brought down by all of what has been going on, but to know that my own parents are spending time laughing it up with the man who—when behind closed doors abuses me—it cuts me like a knife. The only choice I will have is to cut all of you out of my life, along with Steven. I am sorry, but to save myself, so I can save my own children, I will cut you all out of my life, and I mean that."

My father's eyes were stern, when he picked up the phone and asked me for Steven's cell phone number.

Unsure if my father called Steven for my sake or for his own, I quickly dismissed my impulse to judge the intent of his call. If Steven pushed me too far and I cracked, whose responsibility would I be then? Hushing these thoughts away as they surfaced, I committed myself to be grateful regardless of the doubt these thoughts left behind. For what felt like the first time in my life, my father put my feelings ahead of his own.

If You Leave
Me Now

I WAS STUPEFIED WHEN MY parents told me the news. I wondered if they were punishing me, or perhaps they felt as if because Steven and I were getting a divorce, and selling our house, they had no reason to stay. It hurt me deeply to accept the idea that just when I needed my parents the most, they had decided to move out of state.

Like being sucked into a vacuum, my mind swirled with concern over what Steven might do once my parents were gone. Although the parameters my father had drawn with Steven were flimsy, I was grateful that at least they were there. I was sure my parent's decision to move was going to be welcomed news for Steven.

Leslie's husband had longed complained about the traffic in New York. On many occasions he expressed his dissatisfaction for the bustling city streets, as well as for the sheer volume of people that lived in our city. He was adamant about moving to the country, and Leslie was adamant about making him happy. When the two of them announced that they had decided to relocate, my parents agreed to follow them along. When Marc confronted our father about his decision, his remark was, "You're sister needs us. You know her husband doesn't have a job. How is she going to make it without us there watching over her?"

Accustomed to not feeling worthy of my parent's concern, I was not entirely shocked by the news. Like wasps that had been trapped inside a glass jug, my emotions felt stuck, while at the same time wanted out. I felt like a misfit sitting there in my parent's home quietly, listening to their future plans. Nothing made any sense. My father and Leslie's husband barely spoke to one another. A long-standing feud between them had been the cause of many blow-ups in the past. I was dismayed by my father's justifications when Marc pressed him to explain his decisions.

"Dad, you are seriously going to move away from Lisa and I, and to another state, so you can live with a man you can't stand?" Marc asked.

"I can't let your sister move away with her husband. He'll never take care of her the way she deserves," our father replied.

Like bees were stinging the insides of my ears, it was difficult to sit still and hear what my father was saying. Far along in my recovery by now I could feel my mind struggling with the idea of accepting that my parents had the right to do what they wanted, in spite of how I felt about it. The cold hard fact of the matter was, that I was not my father's responsibility, but--nor was Leslie.

I sat quietly listening to Marc's long list of reasons for why my parents should not move away. Almost frozen by the dialogue that was taking place in my mind, I stayed aware of my emotions and did my best not to attach myself to them. When Marc tabled the topic of conversation my way and asked me directly,

"Lee—do you think mommy and daddy should move away from us?" I didn't answer immediately. There, in those silent moments right before I opened my mouth and offered my answer, I could feel my brain stretching to reach for healthier thoughts than I had ever known before.

"Marc you have every right to be upset over the idea that mom and dad are moving. And mom and dad have every right to move regardless of how you and I feel about their decisions. I am not particularly thrilled that they are choosing to move now, but I do know they have the right to live their lives the way they want to. I prefer not to impose my wishes on them, and instead wish them all the luck in the world, in spite of how I feel about the matter. This is about them and it's not about us," I said.

Marc's face was twisted with disgust.

"Are you out of your mind? Are you telling me you think its okay that mommy and daddy run off and follow Leslie and her husband off to another state? Are you telling me, you think it's a good thing that daddy is going to have to live with a man he can't even stand to look at? How the hell is that going to work?" Marc asked.

Marc's concerns were valid. My father and Leslie's husband were open about their mutual dislike for one another. On the surface, their decision to move seemed ridiculous. But I also knew that how I felt about their decision was irrelevant.

"No, I am not saying I agree with their reasons for moving out of state. However, I do understand that I have no right to coerce mommy or daddy into doing what I would like them to do. That would not be fair. This is their life, and they have the right to live it anyway they choose," I said, calmly and collectively seated across the table from both my dad and Marc.

My heart was breaking. I could feel it fill and then burst--fill and then burst. If it were not for my being mindful of the fact that I was in the process of debunking the habitual grids of dysfunctional thoughts that had been programmed into my brain since I was a child, I am sure my response to Marc would have been much different. If I was ever going to fully heal, it was imperative that I be able to remind myself to not always trust my brain. Yes, my heart was breaking, but that was only because I had been conditioned to believe that if my parents loved me, they'd do what I wanted them to do. Mindfully recovering from codependency made me feel like I was on some kind of a recognizance mission meant to secure my true self—a self I had only a shy concept of—yet.

One Day At A Time

I DREADED THE MOMENT STEVEN would discover that my parents had decided to move out of state. I knew he'd find innumerable ways to rub my nose in this shit I could not name. It was impossible to understand why it was my parents felt the need to move at that time, in light of how turbulent my life had become. Deep within me raged a sad stock feeling. Somewhere between wanting their love, percolated a disdain for needing their love at all. My parents could 'see' Leslie, and they could not 'see' me. Nothing had changed much since I was ten at all.

I wanted terribly not to hate my parents for moving out of state, and could hear my spirit struggling to accept their decision to go. As if I had an angel on one shoulder and a devil on the other, and as if the angel could only whisper while the devil could only scream, it was impossible for me not to hear the devil on my shoulder shouting, "Hey mom and dad—fuck you!"

I was alone now, in this muck and this mire. And truer, it was becoming crystal clear that I had always been one who stood alone. In all the illusions and the fantasies my 'hungry for love' mind surmised, the reality was I had always been a forsaken creature. Reality yanked heavy drapes of illusions off of my soul, and began a sloughing of dead spiritual skin, as an awareness of self began to grow.

My parents were leaving me in New York, amidst the filing of police reports, court dates, and orders of protection, to go and watch over my sister and her family in another state. Life long fears had been laid to rest. Always having been one who wondered what would occur if I ever allowed my family to see *me*, I now knew for sure, that whether I smiled or if I cried, it wouldn't have mattered in the end.

With my parents now gone, Steven would be out for blood. I was not surprised the first time he said,

"See—even your own parents don't give a shit about you. They left you behind. Do you think your parents really believe you are in danger? Your parents left because they know you're full of shit Lisa. You deserve what you get for pulling our family apart. They can't stand you— that's why they left. Even your own father told me not to be too good to you. And your mother, she thinks you're selfish. She told me that herself."

Steven was unaware that his comments were doing more good than harm. He was helping me cut the last bits of ties I had to any illusions I had left about my family. Coming to terms with the fact that they were not going to support me in any way during my divorce, uncluttered my thinking. Like a blade that was being sharpened, Steven's remarks only helped me accept the fact that my life was my responsibility. Deeper, I needed to somehow ease into accepting my parents perceptions of my life and me, so that anger and fear would not be able to weigh me down during what I knew was going to be a trifling time unwinding my marriage to Steven.

"My parents left Steven, because they don't like coloring outside of the lines. My parents left because they cannot handle chaos. My parents left because they see Leslie as weak, and they see me as strong. My parents didn't leave because they don't care what happens to me. My parents left because they don't know 'how' to care about me, because I taught them to believe I never needed anything, and that's okay. One day I will finally be free of you and your small-minded thinking. One day my life will be my own. One day you and all this dysfunction will be behind me. One day what you think won't matter much to me at all. In so many ways Steven, for me—that day has already come. This is my life, and it's high time I started creating and living my own reality. And you know what Steven? I am beginning to think, that it's going to be a whole lot easier for me to figure out what I want, with my parents gone anyway."

As Steven's face melted from infuriation into bewilderment, I began to get the feeling his mind had blown a fuse. And when Steven sucked his head back into alignment with his spine, and said,

"You're nuts Lisa, ya' know that. You sound like a whacka doodle. What the hell are you talking about? Reality? What kind of bullshit are you talking about now?" I didn't flinch.

As my awareness of self grew, so did ideas about self-responsibility. It wasn't my parent's responsibility to hold my hand during this divorce. I did this. I wanted to marry Steven, and now I wanted to divorce him. These were my choices, and ultimately I was responsible for the decisions that regarded my life, in spite of how anyone else felt about those decisions. Deeper, I was beginning to really understand, that my parents had just the same rights. Deeper, I was beginning to accept that no one on this planet had to agree with anything I decided to do. This life experience truly was my own, and it was up to me to decide what kind of life experience I wanted to live, and the only way to do that, was to let go of any immature expectations I had of others, and simply let go.

Molding A
Future Reality

I DIDN'T LIKE BEING AT home when the real estate agents brought buyers by to inspect our house. Aware of how uncomfortable my children might be with strangers poking their heads inside of their bedroom closets, I made it a point to be out whenever Steven showed the house. With every new perspective buyer that made an offer on our house, reality seemed to become more 'real'. Soon our marital home would be sold and our lives would be forever changed. As unknowns seemed to mock me like cackling jokesters in my head, it was a struggle not to fall victim to the anxiety fear sometimes created during those times.

To help combat anxiety, I joined a local gym and began an exercise regimen. I found that sitting still only increased the tension I felt in my body. When I was a young child I enjoyed physical activities, like bike riding and swimming. I picked up my first barbell when I was sixteen. A few years later my love of physical activity took a harrowing turn, when I became addicted to exercise and to food. Low self-esteem made it impossible for the tender mind I had then, to be able to comprehend ideas about moderation. Hungry for love, and angry I needed love at all, I overate and then punished myself mercilessly with exercise. Aware of the unhealthy relationship I once had with exercise and food, I stayed mindful of my objective at the time. Exercise was to help me reduce anxiety, and was a way that I could love my self during a difficult time in my life. Awareness itself helped me maintain control over a dynamic that once could have destroyed my life.

As a soon to be divorcee' I could feel the tug of war between the old and the new taking place on the field of my mind. Thankful for all the lessons I had been learning recently, I gave myself permission to enjoy the way exercising made me *feel*. Aware that my cells ghosts had tied exercise to self-loathing, sabotage and punishment in the past, I cautioned myself to take things slow.

I was doing lunges at the gym when a short stout woman approached me and asked if I were a personal trainer. I was surprised by her inquiry and actually laughed in her face when she asked me her question. When the woman's face remained firm, a light bulb lit up in my head. I shook her hand, and thanked her for what I considered to be a compliment, and then hurried myself out the gyms front door. When I got home I flipped on the switch to my computer and began researching training programs for personal trainers.

My heart pounded excitedly as if my spirit were saying, "Yes—yes—yes." It all seemed to fit well into my wants as well as my needs. I wasn't sure where I was going, but I was sure about how I wanted to do whatever needed to get done. I knew I wanted to raise my children. I knew I wanted to be the one to pick them up from school and to cook their nightly meals. I knew I wanted to spend as much physical hands on mommy time with my children as possible, even though I would be working. As a personal trainer, I could make a decent amount of money in a short period of time, and even set my own schedule.

As interested buyers haggled over dollars and cents with Steven and the real estate agent, like a mouse who is hungry for cheese, I burnt the night oil studying my personal training course outline textbooks, and within a relatively short time, I completed three different certification programs. With my certifications in hand, I approached the owner of the gym I had recently joined, and asked him for a job as a trainer in his gym. He hired me on the spot.

It Is What It Is
And Its All Good

I T DIDN'T SEEM REAL. When Steven told me the real estate agents had found a buyer for our house, I wasn't sure if I wanted to jump for joy, or roll into a ball and cry. Life seemed to be changing with every blink of my eyes.

"This is really going to happen Lisa. You and the kids are going to have to find a place to live. When things get tough for you, always remember, it's your fault. You brought this shit upon yourself. We had it good, but no, you weren't happy Lisa. Everything was about your feelings, your feelings, your feelings," he said, mocking me in a whining high-pitched voice, in front of my children, the day he broke the news to us.

Although Steven's words were full of sarcasm, he was right. Growing ever more comfortable with my reasons for wanting a divorce, Steven's maleficence no longer controlled me the way it had once. He was correct on every count, and had it not been for his venomous intent, I might have actually stood there and cried. Things were going to get tough for me. I did bring this upon myself. The decision to get divorced was mine. We did have it good, and this was all about my feelings. I was miserable married to Steven. I was so miserable in fact, my body was failing because of the stress my marriage was causing.

"Okay Steven, thanks for giving us the news. Sorry, but the kids and I have plans. We are going to the beach with Rosey and her kids, so we really don't have time to stand here and talk," I said, hoping to douse Steven's need to continue pouring on the gasoline, as I bustled the kids down into the playroom, and out into our garage.

It was important that my kids and I have fun that day. Our lives were about to change dramatically, and I wanted nothing more but to give them a little reprieve from the dizzy spells our lives had become. Intentionally more present than I had perhaps had ever been, my kids and I dug holes to China and played Frisbee in the sand. It felt good to let go of worry for a little while and detach from giant sized fears of the unknown.

After the beach, Rosey and I put some hamburgers and hotdogs on the grill in her yard for the kids. Rosey's yard was like a resort. Rosey loved palm trees. In fact she loved them so much, her husband planted a bunch of them in her yard, and had an underground heating system put in to keep the trees roots from freezing during the winter months. Rosey's in-ground pool had a slide, and a hot tub too.

As if I were that fly on the wall, many times that day I stopped and took mental inventories. Slowly slipping away from somewhere deep within my being was my habit of feeling consumed by circumstances and people I could not control. I was learning to let go bit by bit, of ideas and concerns that were beyond my reach. My house had been sold, and there was nothing I could physically do to change what had already been done. But as moments past that priceless day, I consciously made choices to laugh, and to play.

Lisa A. Romano

It was getting dark. Rosey was inside cleaning the kitchen and I was outside hosing off ketchup and mustard from her wrought iron patio furniture. My back was to the pool, when I noticed how unusually quiet the yard had suddenly become. Just then I turned to check on the kids.

If my heart were a balloon it would have burst open wide. Rosey's three children and mine, were all sitting in the hot tub quietly giggling. They were each sipping on cans of juice that had been dressed to impress with tiny colorful paper cocktail umbrellas. The expression of ease on my children's faces made my heart swell with peace. Touched deeply by the contented vision of my children, tears began to flow from my eyes. As if my shoulders suddenly had wings, and the weight of the world had finally been released, my heart soared like it hadn't done in many years. It wasn't long before Amanda noticed me noticing them.

"Mommy, are you crying?" Amanda asked.

"Yes baby doll I am crying. But these are happy tears," I said, as I threw my head up at the sky and giggled from my toes as tears continued to stain my pink face.

Learning To Follow
What Feels Good

I T WAS LATE, AND the sun was now sleeping. My kids didn't want to go home. They wanted to stay and play in the hot tub, and continue sipping iced tea and juice from rainbow colored straws. If I didn't have to work the next morning, I wouldn't have insisted we leave.

As I was packing beach toys and loading them in our van, I noticed a large disabled truck on the corner of Rosey's block. Because the truck had blocked the entire cross section of the road, I would be forced to make a left out of her driveway instead of a right, and towards a route that was unusual for me to travel on my way towards home.

I met Georgia when I was about thirteen years old. Around that time I joined the local volunteer ambulance corps just so I could gain the credits I needed to fulfill a community service requirement that was part of my Freshman High School curriculum. Georgia was the youth squad coach at the ambulance corps and she lived directly around the corner from Rosey. My new route home unexpectedly took me past Georgia's quaint powder blue shingled home, the one I had visited many times when I was thirteen.

As I made a left onto Georgia's street, visceral happy feelings began to surface within me. Georgia was more than inviting when Rosey and I were kids, and it was not uncommon for her to ask the members of her teams to visit her at her home if we were ever down in her part of town. Georgia was a childless woman, who had dedicated her life to helping kids stay off the streets. Georgia could never have known that the little girl I was when we met had held a gun against her head just a year before our introduction.

When I was twelve years old, I had been bullied so severely, that I contemplated suicide. By the time I met Georgia, I was in freshman year of high school, and had miraculously made friends with Rosey and another girl named Karen. All three of us were members of Georgia's competing youth squad team. Georgia's direction, her nurturing ways, and her attention to our youth squad group, in addition to her faith in me as the captain of her competing team, was paramount to the way in which my life continued to unfold at that time in my life.

As fond memories began to parlay, my eyes were drawn to a real estate sign that was hanging on the lawn of an old, beat up, aluminum sided house. It was black and white, and had an overgrown front yard. The white tin picket fence was rickety and rusted. A huge tree was rotted from its hull, and its barren limbs hung over the house like spooky arms. From the front of the house, you could see weeds that were waist high had covered the rear yard. The wood door to the garage was hanging off of its mangled track. The front porch screen was torn, and one of the windows to a top floor bedroom had been shattered. The concrete driveway was cracked and it was uneven.

"Mommy why are you stopping?" Max asked, as I dug my hands deep into my handbag in search of a pen.

"I just want to find out how much this house is selling for guys—give me a minute. We'll be home soon," I said.

I scribbled the number of the real estate agent down on my hand with a make up pencil. I couldn't find my pen amongst the baby wipes, pacifiers, and tubes of sunscreen I had thrown into my bag that day on our way to the beach. On the drive home, my eyes kept being drawn to the sparkly blue line of thick numbers that rested on the top of my steering wheel.

Before going to bed, I called and left a message for the real estate agent whose name was listed on the sign that hung in front of the old, beat up black and white home. The following morning the agent and I met, and by the time our meeting was through, I had written him out a check that would ensure he would no longer show the house to any new buyers.

Although the house needed repair, it was a home I knew I could buy out right with the moneys I was going to receive from the sale of my marital home. Without the burden of a mortgage over my head, I was fairly certain that with the money I was making as a personal trainer, I was going to be able to give my children a life we could all enjoy—one day.

Change

MAX AND AMANDA DIDN'T jump for joy when I told them I was planning to move us all into that old beat up house. Max seemed the most perturbed by the news. He had understandably grown comfortable with his custom built digs, and was wrestling with the fact that he'd soon have to let it go. Max enjoyed being the kid who lived in the coolest house on his block, who routinely had his yard filled with neighborhood children. His new home could fit inside one of the rooms he was leaving behind. It was impossible for him to embrace the idea of moving with any sense of excitement. Max was rightfully angry, confused, and sad.

Amanda offered me no protest when I told her the news. As always, my middle child was more concerned with not upsetting me, than she was about her own feelings about what was happening in our lives. Regardless of how often I assured Amanda that I was fine, and that she didn't need to worry about her mom, she did anyway. While Max grew angrier by the day, Amanda instinctively did what she could to grease the tight emotional gears our changing family dynamics had become. Her concern for me, concerned me greatly.

"I am so happy we are going to live around the corner from Rosey mommy," is what she said when I told her I was going to buy the black and white house.

"Don't worry. I know we can fix it up, and make it pretty," she also said.

Grateful for Amanda's tender heart, and her ability to empathize with her mother's overall good intentions, was often times overshadowed by the fear that perhaps Amanda would one day resent being the 'perfect one' when she was, when she was a little girl. Amanda and I had a bond I had never witnessed before in other mother daughter relationships. She was my daughter, but in so many ways she was also a comforting encouraging, and understanding friend.

Niccole was a baby, and like a leaf caught in the wind, had little choice but to follow her families trailing current. My heart felt heavy, like it had swallowed a brick, whenever I noticed confusion creep across my little ones brows. A pixie kiss, or a mama bear hug were often the best I could do to ease the bedazzled heart of my littlest one. Grateful however, for how simple she was to please, I found myself comforted by being able to turn her puzzled frowns upside down with either a smile or a wink.

Aware that if nothing changed, then nothing would change, was as bitter a pill to swallow, as it was sweet to gulp. Determined to ensure my children had the greatest chances possible of being free of codependent thinking in their own lives, first required that I break all the rules and ideas about life, that I once taught them to believe in. Unaware as a young wife and a mother, I failed to comprehend how ill the examples for love were, that I was setting for my children as they grew. I falsely conditioned my children to disown their own needs for the sake of keeping others calm, happy, and content. What I once presumed was a proper and appropriate way to live my life, was in truth a blue print for self-destruction. Sucking up the guilt while at the same time struggling to cling to hope, felt like a croc had pulled me underwater, and had me locked in a death roll that only allowed for momentary reliefs of air.

With the sale of my children's home imminent, and the move into their new home just on the horizon, I found myself feeling lost in states of emotional limbo. In my minds eye I envisioned myself floating in a dark oblivion desperately and repeatedly reaching to grasp for walls I could not find. In disorienting moments like these, it was hellish to force my mind to think above the intense emotionalism that consumed my being. Change, a necessary requirement of codependent recovery, turned my soul inside and out. Surrender and acceptance, also requirements of codependent recovery, many times were not the reinforcements I hoped they would be.

When One Door Closes Many Doors Open

I N THE PAST LESLIE had worked for a real estate attorney named Tom. Tom agreed to represent Steven and I at our homes closing, as well as represent me at the buying of my new home. Like a steamroller, Tom was just the aid I needed then, to help keep me on track and on a steady course. A savvy esquire, Tom made sure the money that I received at the closing of my marital home was written and divided into checks I was going to need to buy my new home, so to keep the transitions seamless.

The many nerves in my body felt like they were jumping off of cliffs that day. And although I felt very lead and directed by our attorney Tom, the pulling apart of what was once so enmeshed made me feel on edge. I hyperventilated more than once that afternoon in the small, cramped and stiff room our real estate closing took place in. My life was being shuffled around like the loose pieces of paper it had become, and it was suffocating to notice how little the professionals in the room seemed to care.

Like I was amputating one leg for the sake of the other, I could only pray that in time that my divorce, the selling of our home, and the splitting of our family would eventually prove to be worth the pain. I knew I was where I needed to be, but that knowing did little to alleviate my mounting anxiety and sudden doubts.

The chairs in the room were made of a black fabric. Uncertain if the stress of the day had caused my period to be exceptionally heavy, or if I was just having an unusual cycle, I was mortified when I realized I had bled straight through my maxi pad, my pants and even onto my seat. When I rose to my feet and excused myself, I could feel a rush of blood pass through me like a stream. I hoped none of the others in the white stuffy room would need to take my place while I was gone.

Within a few hours a huge piece of my old life was gone. After the meeting was through, Steven and I stood outside of the tall office building and spoke civilly to one another for the first time in many months. Still reaching for walls, I could feel myself almost wishing I could throw my arms around Steven and collapse in his embrace. I knew better than to reveal my vulnerable side to Steven however. He had a habit of pulling me in when I was down, and throwing me away when I was up.

"Take care of yourself," I said to Steven as I turned and walked away. I was hunching to get into my car, when I glanced over at Steven for a final time. Our attorney Tom had exited the building and he and Steven were exchanging mannerly handshakes when I noticed them. Steven had a look of shock upon his face, and seemed to be smiling as if only to be polite. Without warning my chest let out a burly moan, and my eyes began to cry as I pulled my car door closed and slipped into the drivers seat. I punched the button down hard that locked my car doors shut, and fiercely strapped my seatbelt into its buckle. And as Steven glanced over his shoulder to watch me pull away, I could feel my heart leaving a trail of shattered dreams behind.

Adjustments

MAX REFUSED TO BE present on the day the moving truck arrived to help transport all of our things to our new home. He also refused to sleep in his new abode on the day we moved in. In fact, it took Max a number of weeks before he was able to bring himself to the point where he was comfortable enough to try and settle into his unfamiliar surroundings. Rosey was kind enough to open her home to him, until his anxiety about our move eased.

Amanda chose to sleep out at Rosey's for a number of nights as well. But unlike her brother Max who was open about his animosity about the divorce, in the early days, Amanda tiptoed unnecessarily about her wishes to sleep at Rosey's. Fearful my middle child might be getting caught between concerns for her father as well as her mother, I did what I could to goad her into having fun when the opportunities presented themselves.

"Amanda, yes of course you can sleep at Rosey's. One of the major reasons I decided to buy this house was because it was so close to Rosey's. And Rosey is totally fine with you and Max going there when you want to—so go and have fun. I will be fine," I would say to Amanda, hoping to squelch any doubts she may have had about leaving her mommy and baby sister alone.

"But what about you and Niccole mama? What are you going to do while Max and I are at Rosey's," my daughter Amanda would ask.

"Niccole and I are going to watch video's and then go to bed early sweetie. Don't worry. It's my job to worry about you, and Niccole. It is not your job to worry about me or your sister," I would say.

Steven was coming undone. Weeks after the kids and I moved into the house, Steven had begun what could only be described as a psychological war against me. From dozens of cellphone calls a day, to the countless number of times he drove in circles around the shopping center where I worked, Steven was making it obvious he was having a hard time processing his feelings.

Steven approached me one afternoon as I was leaving the health club where I worked. His hair was unruly and his clothes were dusty. He was wearing his worn out blue denim work pants, construction boots, and a soiled dark t-shirt. My heart began to beat quickly when I first saw Steven begin to make his way towards me. A friend I had known since grammar school was also in the small shopping center parking lot. I thought little about it when my friend called out to me and said 'hello.' The following day at our children's school, this friend told me that she was concerned for my safety. "Lisa it's none of my business, and I hope you won't think I am being nosy by saying this, but yesterday I was really nervous for you. The look on your husband's face scared me. He looked like he was really pissed off at you, and like any minute he was going to pounce on you or something. Just so you know—I didn't leave that parking lot until I knew you were okay, and I saw you get into your car and you drove away. Listen, if you ever need anything, don't hesitate to call me, and I mean that. Just be careful. You never know what is going on in his head," she said.

I was lost for words when she addressed me. A large part of me appreciated her concern and I was thankful someone who had nothing to do with what was going on in my life had validated my fears. But a deeper part of me worried that maybe Rosey and my old schoolmate Christine had serious reasons to be concerned. So accustomed to feeling lost in the space between what my instincts told me were right, and the fear of making others angry about what my gut was telling me, I wondered if perhaps I wasn't seeing what I needed to see. Overwhelmed by fretting about what all these new unsettling changes might be doing to my children, coupled with trying to acquire clients so I could pay my bills, in addition to the physical exhaustion I was feeling as a result of the ongoing scraping, wallpapering, spackling and painting I was doing on my own in my new home, it was possible I may not have been psychologically capable of being able to worry about my physical safety at that time. As I knocked these wonders around in my stuffed mind, I could feel anxiety wanting to blow the top off of my head.

In addition to experiencing a rough transition into our unfamiliar home, Max was having a trying emotional time adjusting to his new school. My son—the new kid, and worse—the *public school kid* who was now trying to acclimate into a catholic schools seventh grade class environment, found himself being targeted unfairly by a bully named Ryan. When Ryan jumped Max from behind one afternoon after school, my son managed to wrestle Ryan to the ground and beneath him. Once Ryan was on his back, my son straddled him and then punched him in his face. When the squabble was through, my son walked to my car and told me what had happened. A stream of emotions welled up within me. Amongst the never ending gulfs of sadness, guilt, remorse, pity and anger, I could feel my heart screaming,

"God damn this bullshit! My son does not deserve this nonsense!" In moments like those, it was difficult not to wonder if perhaps Steven was right. Maybe I just should have sucked up my own unhappiness, and made the best out of my blood sucking marriage.

Journaling kept me grounded like an old oak tree. And as the gale like winds of change barreled down on my family's lives, writing allowed me to ease back into calmer states of being whenever I felt like my feelings were beginning to overwhelm me. Keeping my eye ever focused on the goal, I consciously forced myself to point my attention in the direction of what my overall well meaning intentions were and had been since I began what was turning out to be, the greatest challenge of my life. As a mother, I needed to know I was doing everything in my power to assure the chains of codependency were being broken, at least in my children's lives. It was not my intent to cause my children harm. In spite of this knowing however, guilt and self-doubt often times made sticking to awareness and to changing my thoughts a harrowing task.

Learning To Accept Help and Setting Boundaries Along The Way

"THIS IS WHERE YOUR mother expects you kids to live? This is a shit house. You poor kids," Steven said to Max as he let my son out of his car after one of their afternoon visits.

My heart bled when Max told me what his daddy had said. It was like coughing up rusty nails when I managed to reply to what my son had shared.

"Max, I am so sorry that daddy was unable to hold his tongue. I am sorry that what he said hurt you, or perhaps made you feel badly about where we live now. I want you to know that your father was wrong for saying that to you. But right now he is a vey angry man. And unfortunately he is not thinking very clearly. He really wants to punish me, not you. I am sorry you are in the middle of this nonsense Max. I cannot control what comes out of your father's mouth. If I could, I would for your sake. I am so, so, sorry," I said.

In many ways Steven was right. Our new house, in comparison to the one we had sold was a shit house. Everything about our old home was new, while every aspect of our new one was dated. From the rotten wood porch, to the rusted cast iron radiators that sat like metal garbage cans in every room of the house, I was well aware of what our new life looked like from a physical perspective. Hoping my children would be able to believe in what I was doing, was asking them to walk by faith and turn away from what was in sight.

I had always been the kind of being who found it impossible to ask for help. Needing was not an emotion that was very much valued in my childhood home. Rather I found odd splinters of worthiness whenever I was able to disown a need I had had as a child. Learning to *not* need was like learning to breath under water. It didn't feel natural, but it was the only way to survive.

With the last bits of money I had received from the sale of our marital home, I hired a contractor to do the required renovations on my new house. Every last dime I had went towards paying the contractor to re-vinyl my homes siding, to install a new roof, and to replace all the windows. This work was aside from the internal labor I was doing on my own, like spackling and painting.

When the plumbing contractor I also hired told me he was going to need an extra seven thousand dollars to finish the job he had started, I panicked. My pockets bare as the result of paying the home improvement contractor, I had no idea where I was going to come up with the money to pay the plumber. The thought never entered my mind to ask my parents for help. It never entered my mind to ask anyone for help, which is why I felt like I had been sucked into the eye of a tornado when Rosey's husband handed her a white envelope with seven thousand dollars in cash stuffed inside it.

I was sitting at Rosey's kitchen table. My eyes were red and swollen. My legs were scraped and scratched. The day before I had seven stitches sewn into the fleshy part of my left palm, the result of struggling with an uncooperative curtain rod. Like a cannon that was ready to explode, my soul detonated almost unexpectedly all over Rosey's table. Tuckered out by the umpteen dilemmas that were billowing in my strange life, I found myself incapable of hiding my emotions in that moment. I hated the side of me that was unable to pretend I didn't need help. Even in front of Rosey, in spite of all we had been through in our lives together, it was terrifying to reveal this deep part of myself to her.

"Lisa it's going to get better. You'll see. I asked my husband to talk to the plumber. Maybe we can work something out," she said. Unbeknownst to me, earlier in the day Rosey had called her husband and explained what was going on. When I heard him walk through Rosey's front door, I quickly straightened up and made sure to wipe the tears from my swollen eyes. I thought nothing of it when Rosey got up and met her husband in the foyer to their home.

Sitting there alone at her kitchen table for a while, I did my best to push back the bangs from my face, and to primp my tight and messy pony-tail. Clearing my throat, I practiced seeming together for her husband's sake as much as for my own. When Rosey re-entered the kitchen without him, I was as confused as I was relieved.

"Here—take this," Rosey said, as she pushed a thick white envelope under my sniffling mug.

"What's this?" I asked, trying to make heads or tails out of what was taking place.

"It's the seven thousand dollars you need to pay the plumber," Rosey said, as my spine began to buckle from the wales of my soul.

"Rosey I cannot take this money from you guys. You have helped me enough. Your husband has sent laborers over to my house to help me out—he rewired my entire electrical system, and you have been nothing but one hundred percent supportive of me and my kids. I can't take this from you—I just can't," I said, through broken and split cries of intimidating humility.

"Lisa—would you do this for me if I was in your position, and you were in mine?" Rosey asked. "Lee— take the money," she said.

I never saw her husband Tim. He slipped out the front door as slippery as he had entered through it. I was thankful he had, and sad at the same time too. Tim understood my kind. When I asked Rosey why he had left so soon, she told me that Tim had only mentioned that he had a meeting he needed to get to and could not be late. My gut told me otherwise.

Rosey and Tim's generosity didn't end when the plumber got paid. Not long after I moved into our new house, Steven told me the lease was up on the van I had been driving. When he removed it from my driveway, I was left without a car. The following day Tim showed up on my doorstep and told me he was taking me to look for another car, and that he was going to help me pay for it. When I assured him I would be fine for a while without a car, he made it a point to stress how unrealistic my argument was.

"Lisa, I am in the position to help you. I know how hard this must be for you. You are a very proud woman, and I can only imagine what it must feel like to be in your position. If you were drowning you'd make sure everyone else around you had a life preserver on before you reached for one. I get it. It's hard for you, if not impossible for you to ask for help. But right now, whether you like it or not, you need help. Let Rosey and I do what we can to get you back on your feet," Tim said, as my mind struggled with reaching beyond its need to pretend he wasn't right. My childhood programming had taught me to relate needing and accepting help with selfishness. Correcting my perceptions about accepting help felt like I was climbing Mt. Everest in my mind.

In time my life settled into a much needed and welcomed routine. My client based flourished at the gym where I worked, and all of my children began to do well in their new school. My dominant intent was to ease as much of my children's anxiety about our new lives as possible. Sadly, the more settled my children and me became, the more havoc riddled Steven seemed. Navigating his anger was draining, exhausting and frustrating.

Approximately one year after the kids and I moved into our new home, life was beginning to find its balance. Working seven days a week had paid off, literally. The money I was making as a personal trainer helped me settle many of the bills I had accrued for things like new appliances, and furniture. With life settling into its newness, I felt the need to take Steven to court. Tired of feeling intimidated by Steven's incessant phone calls, insults and threatening body language, I somehow managed to find the wherewithal to define for him as well as for me a new boundary.

After a short hearing, family court granted me my order of protection, and like I had hoped, Steven left me alone. I was grateful for the reprieve. My greatest regret is that I had not sought an order of protection sooner. Learning to enforce my inner as well as external boundaries helped inch my mind further away from the old parts of me that had not yet learned to embrace the idea that I no longer needed to live my life feeling like a victim and clamoring about injustices. Climbing beyond the old thought processes that had me falsely believing that I didn't deserve to be happy, was like running across a field of broken glass. It wasn't easy, and I didn't want to have to do it. But unless I made the trip, I'd never get to the promise land, the one that flowed with inner peace that was the result of self-love. I didn't want to feel like a victim anymore, and whine about why it was I couldn't ever be completely content. I just wanted to *be* happy. Enforcing my right to live a peaceful life by acquiring that order of protection against Steven was a significant sign that I was more ready than ever to take responsibility for my happiness.

Single Mommy-hood and Relationships

I FELT LIKE A GUPPY in a pool of sharks. I hadn't dated since I was twenty-one. I couldn't remember the last adult conversation I had had with a single man, not including Ed. And I wasn't even sure if he was married or not. He never offered the information, and I never asked.

The road back to me has not been without a pothole or two, or maybe three or four, or maybe ten or ten thousand. Because codependency is a dynamic that is most obvious when it is being played out within a relationship, I knew my experiences with men were chances in disguise to help me heal. Aware that Steven was doing all he could to prevent me from moving on, it was more than frustrating when a date I had scheduled needed to be cancelled because my children's father was MIA and could not be reached by phone after he did not show up for a scheduled visitation.

As I peer over my spirits shoulder and through the jagged peephole that is awareness, I marvel at how often times my consciousness has expanded. This admission however, leaves me with an aftertaste. The decisions I have made along the road back to me, although in the moments when I was deciding them felt appropriate, I understand now were only befitting according to whatever my understanding of self was at the time.

Along my journey I have stumbled ferociously down hills I was certain I would never trip upon again. I have dated and trusted characters I was more than convinced were telling me the truth. I have been duped, used, and deceived by men I thought I could trust. When Steven and I first parted I fell for the first single man that crossed my path, and was unaware that the fear of being alone was at the helm of the emotions I believed were romantic. Because this man had so many qualities Steven didn't, I fallaciously presumed he was nothing like Steven. So on guard for signs of passive aggressiveness, withdrawal, aloofness, condescending innuendos and closed mindedness, I was side swiped when I finally came to realize I had mistaken arrogance for confidence, and egoism for strength in the man I dated after Steven and I separated.

That first relationship after my marriage nosedived is one I have fought hard to forgive. That time in my life, when everything I once knew was slipping away, made me feel as if I had been skinned. Everything hurt. Sometimes a kind word was all it took to help ease the pain, even when the words were nothing but bullshit, and somewhere within me I knew something stunk. And because relief was all I was after at the time, I was sometimes not able to think as clearly as I would have preferred. When I needed a tourniquet I reached for a band-aid instead and ignored the blood that was seeping from beneath its small latex bandage. It did not take long for my mind to be able to find the strength to end that destructive relationship. The lessons it taught me about my self, men and codependent recovery were and are priceless.

I have learned many valuable lessons through my experiences with men. The wisdom I have gained has not come without a price. My heart, although I believe has been healed, is not without scars. Ever since I was a little girl I have believed in fairy tale like love. What I failed to correct in my thinking however, was the notion that love found outside of me was the answer to my prayers. Falsely presuming a relationship would ultimately bring me happiness, I dated many years after my divorce under the improper impression that one day my prince would come and bring me love. I incorrectly set my sights on men and relationships and believed that the right relationship would fix whatever was wrong in my life. In so doing, I was unaware that I in fact was reinforcing the very dynamic I had battled so hard to confront and slay. By believing that a relationship was the key to my happiness, was in actuality leading my mind to depend on love that could only be found outside of my self, which only reinforced any unconscious relationship dependency issues I had not dealt with appropriately. Not yet fully as self actualized, as I would have liked to be, I did not completely comprehend that my frivolous concepts about romance were in fact oozing with codependency. Divorcing my codependent husband was only half of the battle I needed to win. I needed to somehow divorce my own codependent mind, and reconstruct a new set of healthy beliefs about relationships and me as well.

When the moment flashed like a bolt of lightning in my mind, and I became aware that one of the main reasons I felt so compelled to date in the first place, was because Steven did not want me to, I came face to face again with a sneaky codependent remnant I had not easily acknowledged before. So fixated on my desire to not allow Steven to control me any longer, it was like breathing noxious gases when I finally realized Steven was still in many ways controlling my decisions. When at long last I asked my self whether I wanted to date or not, I was floored when within me came a sense that all I wanted to do was spend time alone getting to know 'me'. When I let go of needing to prove to Steven as well as to my self that he was not ruling my life anymore, the need to date softened.

In the time I spent alone, I learned to love my self in ways I never had before. With men no longer a distraction or compulsion in my life, my intimate priorities shifted dramatically. I suddenly became content sitting on the couch on Friday and Saturday nights, sipping tea with my dog, while my children either spent time with their father, with Rosey or with friends. I no longer neurotically sought to fill up my alone time with haphazard phone calls to others, or with men who were not worthy of my time. It became easy and welcome to light a sweet smelling candle and to play soft comforting music while soaking in a hot sea salt bath.

Growing comfortable with asking myself questions about the things that I liked to do was like learning to fall in love with a new friend. I had always been a creature seriously intrigued by the needs of others. With more time to think, I was now learning to take *my* needs seriously and that intrigued me. I learned to take naps when I was tired,

Lisa A. Romano

and to walk in the sun as I naturally began to suck up an appreciation for the divinity of nature. Looking up into the sky became a love of mine. Glancing up at the flowing artwork billowy soft white clouds could be shifted my moods into positive streams of thought instantaneously. Connecting to my inner self, made connecting to all that is seem natural and inherent even. Life became about me, myself and I, and I was learning to enjoy that very much.

Leaving My Codependent Mind Behind

WITH MY LIFE FINALLY becoming about me, and with the stress of relationships gone, I found that my mind was able to confront old patterns more easily than ever before. Detaching from others allowed me to find the stillness I needed to confront realities about my self I had been unable to see in my confusing and distracting past. Infused more than ever with a desire to get my thinking straight, journaling continued to help pull me up and over old negative ridges in my minds thought processes.

When I was twenty-one I thought I knew all that I needed to know. Full of unrecognized anxieties, I lacked the awareness or the appreciation of self, and ignored the demons I now wish I had the cognitive skills to confront. As my ability to face my reality enhanced, I began to understand the creature I once was more deeply than ever before. Although the reconciliations I was making in my mind sometimes felt like I was swallowing staples, the eventual calm that showed up within my inner being always made the meals of metal worthwhile.

I married Steven for as many unhealthy reasons as I did healthy ones. I didn't know then, that Steven was rescuing me, as much as I was rescuing him. In all of the fluff that we called love, were a ton of codependent invisible, and intoxicating needs. For many years I had blamed him for what was wrong with us. Heavy was the reality that my thought processes were as ill as his.

I was a vivacious young girl with dreams of true love, who believed that fairy tales could and should come true. I believed love could be magical if the couple considered the feelings of his/her mate important. Never expecting from Steven more than I was willing to give, I presumed my husband would love me the way I loved him. I was filled with disillusionment, and the anxiety it brought along when I began to find the courage to admit to myself, my presumptions about him--about love and about me were wrong.

Like trying to tackle lightning, it was a dangerous thing to feel the feelings I once believed I needed permission from others to feel. In more ways than one, Steven made it clear that to him my feelings did not count. Stuck in the land that only his eyes could see, Steven and I were a husband and a wife that lived oceans apart. And while the distance between us suit him well it made me feel like I was gasping for air, and worse as if the suffocating sense was all in my mind.

I never wanted to leave Steven. I had to leave Steven. Our marriage was quite literally killing me. After many years of interpreting Steven's lack of interest in our marriage as a lack of interest in me, my body had begun to pay the price for all those secret and scary feelings that I did not believe I had a right to feel at all. When Steven ignored my health and my desire to fix the codependent couple we were, I felt forced to make what I considered a life or death decision. If I had stayed married to Steven, I believe my body would have continued to break down and fill with dis-ease until the toxic emotions finally killed me.

On the road back to me I have had moments in which I felt completely overcome by fear. My fears have manifested in many forms. I have obsessed over how I was going to pay for three private school tuitions, braces, and eyeglasses. I have obsessed over how Steven's early rage was going to affect our children in the long run. I have obsessed over relationships, and with the idea of spending my later years alone. I have obsessed over my lawn, my broom closet of a bathroom, and about the shoes on my children's feet. In the early years, there were many nights I fell asleep sobbing while fear beat against the walls of my mind with what felt like heavy wood nail-spiked two by fours.

But as time moved on, and Steven's tongue grew tired and dry from wagging in the wind, and I continued to reinforce personal boundaries, I found my greatest relief as well as strength in letting go. Twelve years later I am happy to announce that Steven and I have both grown from the rubble of our divorce. Although he and I still live oceans apart, the rough waters between us have certainly quieted over the years. I am grateful for the changing of the tides, not only for my children and I, but for him as well.

Dropping The
Hot Coals

A S OF THIS POINT in time, I have yet to tell my parents about the publishing of my first bestselling book, The Road Back To Me. It is most stabbing when someone I know asks me how my parents feel about my work, and I respond with a heavy "I don't know."

So sadly accustomed to feeling out of my parents loop, it has become ordinary for me to feel as if they are not a significant part of my life, or I a noteworthy part of theirs. My parent's decision to move to a different state just as Steven and I divorced, at the time brought back painful memories of feeling invisible to them like I had when I was a small child. If I ever needed a mother and father in my life, it was then. Their decisions left me feeling alone, and worse, like prey. The most disturbing sense that I found myself needing to sooth, was the morbid juice that showed up in my veins when I finally accepted that my parents left knowing that I was being hunted.

It was a mighty emotional hurdle to not attach myself to anger, knowing that my parents were choosing to move regardless of the drama that was unfolding in my life. Aware that my children were ultimately my responsibility, and that my choice to start over was my decision, it was a chore to remind myself that my parents had the right to live where they wanted to live, even if their decision to live in another state, just happen to coincide with my divorce when I needed them the most

On many days I wished that I could call my mom or my dad and vent to them about how exhausted, and fearful I was. Many days I doubted that I would be able to get up the next morning and face another day of unknowns. When my children and I first made our move, Max was having an especially difficult time adjusting to a new school; Amanda was forever trying to take care of my feelings, which concerned me greatly, and the fear I saw in my little baby Niccole's eyes brought me to my feeling knees every time. Stressed to beyond natural limits over how it was I would survive the enormous stressors of my unraveling life, during those early years my heart played volleyball with anger as well as humble acceptance often.

Although the little girl in me in many ways has grown up, the truth is I do not believe I will ever outgrow longing for the parents who could not 'see' me. As if I have in so many ways been forced to raise my self, it has been soul bending at times to accept that my parents preferred disconnection. My truth is and always has been an inconvenient one. Learning to love my parents for who they are in spite of who I wish they had been is one of my greatest emotional victories. No longer a slave to *what if* thinking, I am pleasantly content with what is, and have learned to surrender to the sweetness of acceptance.

In my first book The Road Back To Me, I spoke of a shift that had occurred within me, that in many ways was the catalyst that enabled me to finally publish my work. I never spoke of what that shift was however, and feel it is now the time to do so.

In August of 2010 I underwent what was supposed to be a routine vaginal hysterectomy. While on the operating room table, my heart stopped beating. My uterus was being removed through a small slit in my vaginal wall, which meant my abdomen had not been surgically opened. My surgeon did not know that I was bleeding internally until I flat lined and my anesthesiologist frantically made a rush call for fresh blood he hoped would trigger my heart to begin beating again.

From what my surgeon, anesthesiologist and nurses have told me, I should not have pulled through.

I spent nearly a week in the hospital recovering, and although my mom called on the phone to check on me everyday, I almost wished she hadn't. When I came to understand that my parents were not going to make the two and a half hour drive to visit me in the hospital, I could feel my mind wrestling not to interpret their decision to imply I was not worthy of their love.

Almost as if I was offering my mother absolution, I assured her I was fine and hoped I was able to ease her mind for not being able to make the trip to see me while I was recovering. Beginning to ooze from the knowing that my parents had no intentions of making the trip, it hurt less to absolve my mother than to sit too long in the toxic stinging goo feeling unworthy of a visit from her and my father began to stir. Deciding not to judge their decision stopped my heart from leaking.

The old and familiar negative emotions that began to stir within me as I lay in my hospital bed were like mosquitos. They stung, left welts, and itched. But unlike the unaware little girl I once was, I now knew that scratching that old itch would only make the itching worse. Armed with the fists of iron positive self-talk can be, I reminded myself to choose to let go, rather than to hold on and jump on the merry go round feeling like a victim can be. Pointing the finger at my parent's, and falling back into feeling like they had forsaken me, was like picking up a red, hot coal I had dropped many years ago. I deliberately used the power of my mind to help me to understand that I didn't need them to visit me to make me feel worthy. In spite of how my parents chose to love me, I was worthy. Refusing to feel like a victim, empowered me from within, and helped me understand that I was choosing to love my self.

In codependent recovery I had learned that the way my brain interpreted data, was the core issue I had needed to solve. By not interpreting my parents decision not to come see me as a negative, or to imply that I was unworthy, I had successfully thwarted what in the past would have been the cause of a downward emotional spiral. No longer needing to tell my parents who to be, or needing to have them validate me in order for me to feel worthy, was like choosing a sweet kiss over a punch to the face.

If I had died on that hot day in August of 2010, my story would have died too. All of the tears, the toiling, and the trials would have been for near naught. While I do appreciate that my growth has had positive affects on my children and would have without the publishing of my experiences, had I left this earth that day, I do not believe my personal destiny would have been fulfilled.

The only reason I procrastinated about publishing my first book was because I feared what the telling of my story would do to my parents. Terminally blind to the pink elephants that had trampled upon the ground that was our family's soil, my personal written saga is akin to ripping the corneas off of my parent's eyes. I silently wonder 'now what?' Now what can I say to the parents I adore in spite of their perpetual inability to appreciate the feeling being I am, now that I have told a story they more likely than not, will be unable to accept or even believe?

Codependents to the their cores—my parent's unconscious agenda is to deny reality. The reality being—that their children always had a right to their own realities, and it was their responsibility to teach us to honor our 'selves' rather than to deny our 'selves' for the sake of others needs for illusions and senses of control. By unknowingly infusing me with the sense that I had no right to be who I was—by conditioning me to fear what they thought about me, had programmed me to interpret data in a dysfunctional way. Under the illusion for so long that others had the right to tell me who to be, and too, that I had the right to tell others who they should be, kept me stuck in cycles of toxic emotions that caused me to feel like the world was against me for so long.

Pink elephants can only be seen by those brave and honest enough to acknowledge their stench. In a world of those who have been sadly desensitized to foul smells, or who are unable to see beyond the safety of their cocoons, it is sometimes best to keep the secrets of your senses to yourself. It hurts less to stuff, than it is to be told what you see is all in your head, by those that fate has deemed be the ones who teach you about love and about self. Understanding why I was the way I was, and then deliberately deciding to change my unconscious beliefs about others, the world and ultimately my 'self' had successfully taught me--to grow up.

In spite of all that has been I will take my last breaths telling the world that I am proud of my parents. While I know how absurd this statement will appear to some, the truth is, through my spiritual eyes I am only able to see two adult children of alcoholics who did the best that they could with the tools that they had. My parents were far better parents than their own. In their way, they tried. And for this, I am grateful. I am unsure if the shame-based souls that they are will ever be able to see my heart the way that I can see theirs. And if my parents ever do decide to choose to disown me, because I chose to tell my little girls story, I will love them regardless. I have learned to love in spite of not being loved quite the way I would have preferred, because wisdom has taught me to know the difference between *being* love opposed to being dependent on love, and between loving others, and being dependent on others for love. I am love. I always was love, and this is my reality, today. These days, as the data I receive from my environment filters through the eyes of love, I find that I am more peaceful and serene that I ever have been before.

The Apology

I T DOESN'T SEEM TO matter. Regardless of how much time passes, tears still find their way to the corners of the slits my eyes are. I remember our once magical like life. I remember the extravagant birthday parties, the fancy cakes, and the balloons. I remember the large open rooms of our custom built home, and the warmth of our fireplaces. I remember the excitement in your eyes when it was time to visit Mickey and Minnie Mouse, and the rambling belly laughs you'd spout whenever daddy would do his silly jig on our coffee table. My darlings, I remember and feel it all.

I hurt you--my innocent babies, in more ways than one. And this public acknowledgment is in no way intended to minimize or excuse the turmoil each of you has uniquely endured. I wished, oh God I wished there could have been another way to fix what was wrong. It is unlikely that you will ever be able to fully grasp why I did what I did. I learned to understand that part of what was wrong was the illusions of fairy tales I helped to create in your life, and that the only way towards a healthier life was through the crashing of those illusions.

In this moment, I am engulfed with bittersweet emotions. My higher self urges me to look up, rather than over my shoulder. I feel within me a battle ensue. I want to punish myself for hurting you, as well as to forgive what has been done. It is not an easy thing to do, to accept that my choices, in spite of their holy intentions, have ripped apart you souls.

The four of us have been through innumerable storms together. Often I wondered if I'd lose one, two, or all three of you. Many times it would have been easier for you to walk away from the home I was struggling to re-create, than it would have been to stay and stick it out with me. It was heroic of you to stand beside me through all the trials, the ups and the downs, the hurricanes, and tornadoes too. I would have been hurt, but I would have understood too, if you had left the shreds of a life I was trying to reweave. You did not deserve all that showed up.

I sigh heavy loads of disillusionment and regret. I weep for the mistakes I have made, and for any ill perceptions of the mother I have been, or for the mother I am, that you may hold for me now. My angels, it is my prayer that you know in the deepest parts of your soul, how eternal my love for you is. It is my hope that in the cycle of life that we have experienced together, that the chains of codependency have been broken, and that as a result your future lives as well as the future lives of your children, will have been spared from the ill thought processes the ambiguous disease codependency is.

Know that you are love—you were born out of love—and at your core you are as divine as any star, moon or sun. Know too that your worthiness just is—and is not dependent on anything or anyone outside of the miraculous being that each of you is, and that includes your mother.

A prouder mother I do not believe exists. Max, you have become an open minded, vastly intelligent, soul seeking young man, who is in love with discovering his own truth for his own sake. I adore that about you my son. And please know, that I 'see' you, and that I acknowledge, that of all of my children, because you were my first, you suffered more intensely the effects of the blind mommy I once was. I pray that you have found it in your heart to forgive me, for any of the wounds my unawareness may have caused you.

Amanda, you have always been my German shepherd, my biggest fan, and my greatest supporter. You were always there when others were not. A young teenager yourself, it was you who walked Niccole across the street to Rosey's house all those school mornings, when I went to work early. And it was you who spent all those hours in our little house, keeping her safe while I worked in the afternoons. Without you, I could not have accomplished what I have. Had it not been for your patience and understanding of the delicate situation that had become our frail life, I would not have been able to support the home we all lived in. You are as much a part of any victory our family has had, as I am. You are an angel, and I am so lucky and full of gratitude for the blessing to be able to call *you* my daughter.

Niccole, you never knew about fairy tales. You never knew the joy of large parties, or the excitement of lavish Christmas mornings. You never knew the late night barbeques, or the never-ending stream of family and friends that traipsed through our large double front doors. You never knew a mommy and a daddy that tucked you safely into bed. Your life my dear, was in many ways empty of sugar plum fairies instead. Because our fairy tale life ended just as your life had begun, your life experience has been one that very much lies in contrast to your brother and your sister's once dreamy life.

My heart feels as if it is ripping into shreds. You missed so much. As if you were born in a different place and time, the six years between you and Amanda seemed to warp you into a foreign land. Your life was such a stark contrast from the life Max and Amanda had known. I have wondered often which life experience was worse. Never having known fairy tales, or having the fairy tales you have known, turn out to not be fairy tales at all? I wonder too, if I was able to make you feel safe, and as if your life wasn't missing anything at all? I can only hope, that in all the chaos that ensued after your birth, that I was able to make you feel loved, and secure in spite of it all, because in truth my darling, you were the lucky one. Your life was never--not real.

I am sorry your lives may have been less than you deserved. I am sorry any of what I have ever done has hurt you in any way. I hope from the deepest depths of my soul, you three know how deeply you are seen. I see you, my babies. I see your hearts, your fears, your pain, your sorrow and your disappointments in me too. If there was a way I could erase the pains of the past, and rewrite the story that has been us, I would. But that is not possible. What I can do is begin to tell a different story. I can write about where I would like to see us go. I can write about tomorrow, in spite of our yesterdays, and hopefully instill in you the desire to dream your own dreams no matter what has ever been before.

To my darling children…Namaste…

Can You Hear Me Out There?

I SPENT A LOT OF time alone in my room when I was a little girl. My ability to fantasize helped whisk me away when the density of my physical world got too heavy for my fragile shoulders to bear. I would imagine what it would *feel* like to be swept off my feet by love. I would daydream about being rescued from the callous life I was being forced to live, and *feel* my way into states of emotional bliss. My heart would sing and pound as it visualized with great vigor the pure positive vibrational energy love could be. I would sometimes lay in my bed for hours creating movies in my mind about how it might *feel* to be seen, valued, appreciated, and adored by another.

Decades later, the single mom dating scene seemed to fall short from the movie like versions I had stored away in the vaults of my own mind when I was a little girl. In search of primarily a--*feeling*, one I had no tangible cognition of, was like looking for a *thing-a-m- jig* in a haystack. I didn't know what the *thing-a-m- jig* looked like, but I knew how I expected it to *feel*. If the feeling I thought love was could exist in my mind and in my heart, then I knew it also had to exist out in the world somewhere.

On more than one occasion I was almost convinced that I ought to settle for what was showing up on my romantic doorstep. I wondered many times if the feeling I was searching for was realistic, and wondered if perhaps I had set my standards too high. Unsure if the feeling

I was in search of would appear instantly when I met a new man, or rather if the feeling I was in search of would evolve, I was not quick to end budding relationships, even when a part of me knew on a visceral level that the relationship was one I did not wish to last. No matter how hard I sometimes tried to make a relationship *feel* right, I never could quite quiet the dreams of the goddess within me whose dreams had been birthed so long ago, through the heart of the little lonely girl I once was.

By the time I turned forty-three, I had grown tired of feeling like something was missing in the relationships I had been having. With time marching on and becoming more valuable, I no longer felt willing to waste my time in relationships with men I knew could never bring me the happiness and contentment I was in search of. I made a commitment to myself that I would not begin a relationship again unless I could find a man that had all the qualities I was looking for in a romantic partner. My primary gauge would be the way that the man made me *feel* when I was with him.

Along my life's journey I had learned to appreciate how my unconscious beliefs had dictated the conscious decisions I had made about men in the past. I was aware that unless my unconscious beliefs about what I believed I deserved in a relationship changed, I would never manifest the type of relationship I could hear myself consciously thinking I wanted. Armed with a new approach about romantic entanglements, I decided I had nothing to lose by unabashedly writing out a detailed list that included all the specific qualities I was looking to experience in a relationship. I imagined the universe was all mine, and that it had been waiting my whole life for me to give it a command. Knowing inherently that unless I believed I was worthy of love, a love that was worthy would never show up, I milked in as many ways as I could a deep sense that I was a worthwhile creation who had the right to a love that was authentic, real, loving, kind, and filled me with contentment.

"Dear Universe,

Hey it's me, you know…the girl who is forever searching for answers about this thing or that. I am tired of feeling confused by my relationships with men. I finally know what I want, and what I deserve…so here it goes…I know you're listening. By the time I am forty-five, I want to be in a relationship with a man that makes me *feel* seen. I want to be in a relationship with a man who makes me *feel* as if my feelings matter. I want to *feel* connected, on a deep level with him, and *feel* as if his soul knows mine. I want to *feel* like I can trust this man with all of me. I want this man to *feel* like he can trust me too. I want a partner that I can be silly with, and who won't be afraid to be silly with me. I want a relationship that encourages me to be who I am, and makes me *feel* supported, encouraged, safe, and content. I want to *feel* like the man I am in a relationship with is one my children would be proud of. I want to *feel* like my children accept this man, and our relationship. I want this man to be one who understands how important my children are to me, and who *feels* as dedicated to family as I am. I want to *feel* like this man and I are equals, and that we are in a relationship because we want to be, and not because we need to be. I want this man to be good with his money. I want him to be financially responsible, to be a snazzy dresser, and to smell good. I want this man to be kind, understanding, thoughtful, romantic, and to have an adventurous spirit. I want this man to love to dance too. So if you're listening Universe, I'll be waiting patiently for my order to be fulfilled. You know where to find me.

Believing

M Y THOUGHTS HAD RADICALLY changed in the ten years I was divorced from Steven. Incrementally, bit by bit my beliefs about the world, me and others had improved greatly. I no longer felt like a victim and instead had slowly learned to master my own mind, and learned to *feel* comfortable with taking back the reins of my life. The moment I finished writing that letter of intention to the universe, I filled with a deep sense that I had to do my part to help improve my chances of ever manifesting the type of romantic relationship I had been dreaming about since I was a little girl, with a fluffy pink and white comforter yanked over her head.

I stuffed the letter into one of the many books I had been reading at the time and eventually forgot all about it. The period in my life after I wrote the letter was an odd one. I discovered that I was significantly more aware about the choices I was making not only in relationships, but also about normal everyday life. I found that I was becoming more and more comfortable alone. Detaching from others was something I looked forward to doing. I happily discovered that I could feel joy all by myself and needed no one, not even my children to fill me with deep senses of gratitude.

That time of my life was about deliberate choice making. I began to hear myself asking questions like, "Do I *feel* like I want to go there, or would I *feel* better by not going? Do I *feel* like I want to go to dinner with this man, or do I *feel* I would be happier not going? What would make me *feel* better right now? Do I *feel* like this guy is going to fit into my life's long term plan, or do I *feel* like he will not fit into my long term plan?"

It took ten years for me to learn what it felt like to honor my self. Every scrape, bruise and gash my soul had suffered had taught me well. No longer unconsciously or codependently expecting others or things to make me feel happy, I had finally learned to master my own reality by learning to tune into the self that in the past I had been taught to disown.

In the letter I had written to the universe, I had stated that by the time I was forty five I wanted to be in a relationship that held within it all of dreams my heart had held about love. And if I told you that the man of my dreams asked me out on our first date on my forty fifth birthday, it would be difficult to believe. But as difficult as it might be to imagine, the fact is—that is exactly how my story goes.

About three months before I turned forty-five, I joined a popular and reputable dating website. Done with trying to make the relationships that weren't working work, I made a decision to investigate what it might be like to be coupled with potential partners based upon similar personality traits. A believer in the idea that compatibility is something that runs a whole lot deeper than age, or physical attributes, I was curious about meeting a man who had proven comparable emotional idiosyncrasy's to my own.

A few weeks before my birthday, and as it just so happens also on the final day of my online dating site membership, I received what the dating site calls an *Icebreaker* by a man named Anthony. By that time I was pretty certain I wasn't going to sign on for another three months. The hundreds of profiles I read, and the few men I exchanged emails with had left me feeling disappointed. But when I read Anthony's profile, I felt an immediate attraction that compelled me to whip out the ol' credit card. In order to continue interacting with him, I'd need to purchase an additional three-month membership.

I called Anthony on the same day that he sent me his cell phone number via one of the many emails we exchanged back and forth. The conversation flowed as easily as water does down a stream. Anthony and I spoke daily from that point on until we finally met for dinner on March 2nd. My birthday is March 1st, and had I not intended to spend the day with my three children, Anthony and I would have met for the first time on my forty-fifth birthday.

As cliché as it might sound, I knew the moment I saw Anthony that he was the prince I had been dreaming about since I was seven years old. As if when my eyes fell upon him my spirit were saying, "It's him, it's him…I know it's him," I could feel for the first time in my life what felt similar to the feelings of love I dreamt about when I was a little girl. Unlike any experience I had ever had with a man before, the knowing that welled up within me was from a deep and sacred place. Like the long lost key my souls heart had been searching for, Anthony unlocked doors within me I had only prayed one day might open.

As my relationship with Anthony continued to blossom, I began to understand why I had never found him before. Until I found me, I could never have found him. When I finally learned to believe I was worthy of love, a love that was worthy showed up.

This story is not without a hitch. Although every cell in my being was certain Anthony and I were destined to be together from the first moment we met, he was not as sure as I. Only a year and a half since his own first marriage ended, and newly single from a relationship he had begun soon after he separated from his first wife, Anthony was far from as available either physically or emotionally as I would have liked. Two weeks after he and I met, Anthony told me he was not certain he was ready to commit himself to a 'relationship.' Although my heart was broken, I released any attachments I had created in my mind to him, and eased slowly down heartbrokenness and let go.

A few days after Anthony and I ended our relationship, I felt a deep-seated need to send him an email. In the letter I told him that I respected where he was on his journey, and that I was truly happy we met at all. Grateful that I now knew for sure the feeling I was looking for was real I wrote,

Anthony,

"I am so grateful you and I met. I have to accept where you are right now, and I do. If I can feel this strongly about a man like you, who is not yet ready to move forward in a committed relationship, I can only imagine how truly incredible I will feel when I finally do meet a man who is as ready as I am. I honor and respect your feelings, and have come to the conclusion that you and I might only be destined to be friends. And although I wish you felt differently, I do accept how you feel. If you ever need a friend to talk to, know that I have been where you are, and that I understand. Good luck to you today and always...

Lisa

My heart was racing the moment I pressed the 'send' button. Uncertain how Anthony would interpret the letter, I simply let go of any expected outcomes and tried to move on. I was grateful for where I was on my journey in life. In the days that past after I wrote Anthony that letter, I could hear my thoughts urging me to be kind to myself. Feeling exhausted by the energy it took to surrender and let go of what I was convinced was the love of my life, I took hot baths daily, listened to relaxing music, took yoga classes, and meditated as often as I could. Eventually I reached a place in my heart as well as in my mind that allowed me to fully accept the possibility that Anthony and I might never be together.

It was a chilly March afternoon. I had stopped by to see Rosey. She and I and our daughters were seated in the living room watching CSI. Rosey always loved crime investigative type shows. My cell phone was in my hand when it rang. When I looked down and saw the name 'Anthony' lighting up on my phones screen, I leaped out of my chair and announced out loud to Rosey and the girls,

"Oh my God, Anthony is calling me," and as if I were a boy crazed twelve year old little girl, I ran to Rosey's bathroom and shut the door behind me before I answered the call.

"Lisa…hi it's Anthony. Can you talk?" he said.

If You Can Change Your Mind—You Can Change Your Life

THE FOLLOWING DAY ANTHONY invited me out for a quick bite to eat. Still unsure where his head was at the time, I reminded myself to hold back and allow him to decide in what direction he wanted our relationship to go. If all he wanted was a friend who understood what he was going through, I was willing to be that friend. If instead he decided he was interested in a relationship, I was more than willing to move in that direction as well. Incredibly clear minded at the time, I told myself to accept whatever course our relationship/ friendship took, because either way I was grateful I had met such a man as he, and that the *feeling* I believed love could be, was real.

With my boundaries clear, I found myself wonderfully anxiety free about the future. My goal was to live in the moment and to simply enjoy any time I was able to spend with Anthony. With expectations and attachments off my radar, my time with Anthony felt free, light, and joyful. I could only hope he felt the same.

Within a few weeks of that phone call, Anthony and I gently slipped into a romantic relationship. Out of the friend zone, I cautioned myself to continue taking life's moments spent with him day by day. What mattered to me most was the joy I got to feel when I was with him. Not analyzing every detail of our relationship freed me up and allowed me to be present and connected to the now.

Five months later, Anthony was by my side when I went into the hospital to have that vaginal hysterectomy. I had been having irregular bleeding that included hemorrhaging for many years prior. When my doctor told me he found pre-cancerous cells in my uterine wall, we decided a hysterectomy was in order.

What was supposed to be a routine surgery turned into an unforeseen and harrowing experience. Because my surgeon had decided to remove my uterus through a small incision he had made through my vaginal wall, he did not know that I was bleeding internally because my abdomen was untouched. With my abdomen closed he was unaware that blood had in fact been pooling from the veins and muscles he needed to incise to remove my uterus. None of the doctors or nurses knew my life was hanging in the balance until I flat lined on the operating room table and my anesthesiologist yelled for blood.

As the surgical team frantically scurried to infuse my dying body with fresh blood, my doctors were unsure whether I would pull through. Having lost forty percent of my own blood internally, they could only pray that my heart would have the strength to begin beating normally again once enough new blood was transfused into my blood stream.

Before my surgery began my surgeon assured Anthony the procedure would only last a little over an hour. When instead Anthony sat in the waiting room area beyond two hours, he began to become concerned that perhaps something had gone wrong. When after three hours my surgeons confronted Anthony and told him they were not sure if I was going to survive, he was faced with the enormous responsibility of possibly having to be the one who would have to tell my children that their mother had died.

A few hours later my doctors again approached Anthony and told him I was in a coma on a ventilator and in critical condition. They offered him no guarantees that I would survive. Anthony called Amanda and told her that I was resting comfortably and that he would call her back in the morning. He also told her it would be best for her to come and see me the next day, because it was so late in the evening. Because Anthony did not yet know which way my health would turn, he decided it was best to wait until the doctors were sure what my fate would ultimately be before any of my children, family and friends were told anything about my status.

In the intensive care unit, my surgeon and anesthesiologist assured Anthony there was nothing he could do for me there, and suggested he go home and get some rest. Just before Anthony was getting ready to leave the hospital, one of my doctors noticed how improved my vital signs suddenly seemed, and asked Anthony to stay a bit longer. The doctor wanted to see how well I would do without the ventilator, and he thought Anthony should wait long enough with him to find out.

When I first opened my eyes, I could see Anthony standing to my right. He was rocking gently back and forth when he said,

"Hurry up and get better. I want Sabayon."

Anthony had taken me to one of his favorite Italian restaurants a few months before my surgery. He took me there specifically because he wanted me to try their Sabayon dessert. I surprised him the next time we were together at his home and I made the rich dessert for him in his kitchen. Groggy and in pain, my heart soared when I opened my eyes and saw Anthony smiling down at me and by my side. I remember giggling when he prodded me to make him Sabayon. l had no idea at that time how dangerously close to death I had been just hours earlier.

For the five days that I lay in the hospital bed, Anthony rarely left my side. Each day he found the time to come sit and be with me while I recovered. From the smallest to the largest of details concerning my care, Anthony made sure I received everything I needed.

When my doctors informed Anthony and I that my insurance company was only willing to pay for five days of hospital care, Anthony suggested I go home with him so he could give me the care I needed until I was strong enough to be able to care for myself. Unable to walk, sit, stand or get to the bathroom without aid, I knew the best decision for me at the time was to take Anthony up on his kind offer. My children were being watched over by their father and Rosey, and although I wanted desperately to be with them, I did not want my children to see me in such a fragile state. For the first time in my life, I truly needed physical care, and there was no pretending I was not raw, vulnerable and in need of real help.

The hospital discharged me at ten o'clock in the evening and without any pain medication. When a few hours into the night the pain in my body reached an excruciating level and it I felt like my insides were burning from within. The fire in my belly was so intense my body began to tremble from the pain. Sweating, and overcome with inconceivable pain, I began to weep softly as I slowly reached towards Anthony's side of the bed to ask him to please help me sit up. Immediately Anthony darted to the edge of where I laid and cautiously swooped my dead weighted legs gently off the side of the bed, as he simultaneously eased me to an upright position with his free arm. With tears slowly streaming down my face, I rested my forehead up against Anthony's belly and wept. Anthony offered me no words. Instead he stroked the back of my neck and the sides of my arms tenderly, and let his merciful hands do the talking.

Over the next week Anthony cared for me as if I were made of glass. His keen perceptions alerted him to when my pain was climbing, long before I ever even had to open my mouth. So in tune was my beat with his, the time I spent under his care made me feel like we were dancing a ballet.

A month later I was at home and still healing from the surgery when I picked up a book and the letter I had written to the universe over two years earlier floated to the floor. I felt an immediate need to get off of my feet as I began reading the letter aloud to myself in my bedroom. And when I got to the part of the letter that spoke about how it was I wanted to *feel* about a man in a relationship, my eyes turned into fountains.

I have never cursed what happened to me during my surgery. But I had never quite seen the event as a blessing either. But after reading the letter, I had a much different understanding of my experience. It was because of my surgery that I now believed fully in Anthony's love for me. Because of the compassionate way Anthony had cared for me, I could *feel* in the deepest parts of me-- love. Just as I had asked the universe for, I now could *feel* encouraged, supported and safe, and like my children could be proud of the man in their mother's life. All of the desires that I had requested two years before I had ever met Anthony were now becoming a part of my physical reality. My surgery offered me the opportunity to experience Anthony in a way that I might not had been able to, had it not been for the complications I experienced. And now I knew from the deepest parts of my being that I was experiencing an authentic, romantic, loving relationship. The icing on the cake, was the fact that Anthony asked me out precisely on the day that I turned forty-five.

Living Life
By Design

OUR FIRST HALLOWEEN TOGETHER, two months after my surgery, Anthony and I hosted a Beattle's themed bash. Our guests were required to come dressed as characters from any Beattle's song. Rita the Meter maid showed up, as did Yoko Ono and John Lennon. The Eggmen and a Blackbird or two found their way across strawberry field and onto penny lane as well.

The second Halloween party we hosted together, we decided to throw a seventies hit sitcom television series character theme party. Our guests were asked to pick their favorites seventies hit television sitcom character, and come dressed as that character. Fonzi, and Pinky Tuscadero, along with Mr. Kotter, and members of the Addams family attended the bash. Anthony and I chose the hit show *I Dream of Jeannie* for our inspiration. Anthony wore an authentic air force uniform, and played the role of Major Anthony Nelson while I wore a pink genie costume and played along as Jeannie, his genie who lived in a bottle.

All of our guests went out of their way to entertain our playful request to dress as sitcom characters. Anthony's home was full of characters from the cast and crew of Gilligan's Isle, to characters like Laverne and Fonzi from the show Happy Days. As laughter lit up the room with friendly excitement, and we all danced to disco beats, I remember feeling as if my heart might burst open wide from how good I seemed to fit, in that space and time.

Anthony is generally a quite man. When he grabbed me by the hand and escorted me to the center of the floor, and then reached for a microphone, I was taken aback. Unsure of what he was going to say to our guests, I presumed he was going to thank them all for coming and entertaining our odd party theme requests. Nothing could have prepared me when Anthony said,

"I would like to thank you all for coming, and I would also like to thank my girlfriend Lisa. If it had not been for her, this party would not have gotten off the ground. Lisa has taught me a lot in two years--most of all that there are no coincidences in life. And it is no coincidence that she is dressed like a genie, because she has made all my dreams come true."

Stunned by Anthony's sentiments, I turned to look into his eyes, so I could thank him for being so kind. I presumed Anthony was through with his little speech, but then he said,

"But I have one more wish I would like her to grant me," and then he dropped to one knee and pulled out a diamond engagement ring and said,

"Lisa, will you spend the rest of your life with me?"

Once Upon A Time

ONCE UPON A TIME a little girl made a wish upon a star. That wish came from her heart. It was pure. It was holy. It was divine.

The wish my heart made when I was a little girl was for love. I wished for the kind of love that would fill my heart as well as my home with peace.

When I was a little girl, and I would dream about love, my heart would become full to its brim with immense feelings of joy. Beneath the veil of my fluffy comforter, I would lie in bed and close my eyes and imagine the feeling I believed love could be. My mind would take me away and I would forget that I was not worthy of love. For at least a little while, I would find peace.

Today many of my dreams have already come true. I gleefully announce that the feeling I once imagined love could be is as real as you or I. As if the universe had stowed away all the feelings I ever wanted to experience in some galactic vault, and was waiting for me to finally be allowing of all the wishes I had ever dreamt, my life continues to unfold as if by design. In so many ways I am still that little girl who enjoys wishing on stars. Only nowadays I understand that the universe has ears.

"Happy are those who dream dreams and who are
ready to pay the price to see them come true."
Leon-Joseph Cardinal Suenens

My Life's Passion and Purpose

MY PURPOSE FOR WRITING this book is simple. I am passionate about healing this world in as many ways that I can, and believe that much of the unnecessary pain beings experience is due to conditioned codependent belief systems. I believe codependency is a worldwide epidemic. I also believe that because our schools, homes, religions and societies at large tend to imply that beings should conform to the norms of the particulars mentioned, a major consequence is that individual creativity is stifled, and as a result so too is a beings ability to live life believing in positive possibilities.

Codependency is not a dynamic that is exclusive to beings that are in relationships with those who are addicted. Any time a being is preoccupied with another persons needs, or preoccupied about their relationship with another, to the extent that the worry they experience over the other, or the relationship comes at the expense of self, the dynamic is considered to be codependent. Sadly, many of us have lived, or are running our lives under falsehoods and creating unnecessary pain in our lives because we have been conditioned to believe that our worry over others is normal, and worse--justly and good.

Worry and preoccupation cause blocks within the being. These blocks are felt as stress within the body. When negativity invades the body, creative ability is stifled, and it becomes all but impossible to go within so to be able to visualize the dreams of the heart. Without the love and ultimate acceptance of self, the very connection the being is born with, that allows for the being to activate its creative mind is lost and abandoned. Life then is lived by default, under the rules that have been laid out by those stronger, older and more powerful than ourselves. In contrast, the beings we were born to be were intended to create life deliberately, through the power of our creative minds. Our hearts were intended to give birth to these dreams, and our bodies were intended to be the vessels in which we physical beings got to experience our dreams through while here on this physical planet we call earth.

When homes are run by self absorbed caretakers, whether those caretakers are passively aggressive, verbally cruel, unpredictably explosive, emotionally absent, over-indulging, physically abusive, enabling, perfectionistic, or addicted, the consequences are the same. When children have no other choice but to live in chronic states of stress, connections to self must be abandoned. When a child feels threatened either physically, emotionally, or psychologically, their need to survive takes precedent over dreaming dreams he/she unconsciously fears will never come true. And if dreams are born, they are driven by neurosis and fear, and not by joy.

Chronic stress in a childhood home causes the child's mind to develop patterns of worry. Fearful and on guard for the next attack, the child's mind is forced to develop keen observatory skills. Worrying about others moods becomes a tool for survival. Unfortunately for many of us children who grew up in homes oozing with tension, we lost our way through life, and lost our 'selves' too.

Healing from within is possible. Desire to know and to ultimately love and accept self drove me to continue digging deeper for greater understandings. I have known the pain that comes from loathing the self. I understand the temptation suicide can be, when breathing has become like inhaling fiberglass. I know the heaviness that is depression, and the skin infesting feeling anxiety produces. I know the brutal club punishing self-talk can be upon the terrain of the mind, and the bloodthirsty ache that is the result of believing in ones own unworthiness.

"Courage is resistance to fear—mastery of fear— not absence of fear." Ralph Waldo Emerson.

Change, a necessary requirement of healing the mind is often times riddled with fear. But fear is no reason to give up on believing that the life one dreams about attaining one day will be a reality.

"Imagination is more important than knowledge. Knowledge is limited." Einstein.

Belief that one day my life could and would be different fueled me to get back up, when after I had fallen.

"Our greatest glory is not in never failing, but in rising every time we fail." Confucius

Without desire, my life could not have become the joy filled and loving experience it has.

"There is one quality in which one must possess to win, and that is the definitiveness of purpose, the knowledge of what one wants, and a burning desire to possess it." Emerson

Within us all is the seed of greatness. Some of us have more dirt covering those seeds than others. It matters not the amount of dirt that sits upon our seeds. The matter is the seed.

"It's not that I am smart. It's that I stay with my problems longer." Einstein.

Only when I am asked to explain how it was that I made it through those early years after my marriage ended, do I stop and begin to realize just how far I have come, and just how many mountains I have climbed. From the time I was a child, within my chest was a beating heart that beat the drum of desire. I desired one thing most of all, and that thing was—peace. My heart would not rest until within my being I found peace.

"We can never make peace in our outer world unless we first make peace in our inner world." Dalai Lama

"There is no need for temples, no need for complicated philosophies. My brain and my heart are my temples. My religion is kindness." Dalai Lama

"As human beings our greatness lies not so much in being able to remake the world—that is they myth of the atomic age—as in being able to remake ourselves." Gandhi

If I have learned anything in this life it is this—all love starts with self love…and self love comes only by way of embracing the courage to tell the truth, even if that truth topples over a few apple carts along the way.

"This above all—to thine own self be true." Shakespeare

Namaste…